LABORING TO LEARN

LORNA RIVERA

Laboring to Learn

WOMEN'S LITERACY AND POVERTY
IN THE POST-WELFARE ERA

UNIVERSITY OF ILLINOIS PRESS
URBANA AND CHICAGO

Sections of the epilogue have been previously published in "Social Inequality, Education, and Social Mobility," *Democracy & Education* 15 (2): 34–38.

Manufactured in the United States of America
1 2 3 4 5 C P 5 4 3 2 1
∞ This book is printed on acid-free paper.

Library of Congress Cataloging-in-Publication Data
Rivera, Lorna.
Laboring to learn : women's literacy and poverty
in the post-welfare era / Lorna Rivera.
p. cm.
Includes bibliographical references and index.
ISBN-13: 978–0–252–03351–3 (cloth : alk. paper)
ISBN-10: 0–252–03351–5 (cloth : alk. paper)
ISBN-13: 978–0–252–07555–1 (pbk. : alk. paper)
ISBN-10: 0–252–07555–2 (pbk. : alk. paper)
1. Women—Education—United States.
2. Welfare recipients—Education—United States.
3. Educational equalization—Education—United States.
4. Literacy—United States.
I. Title.
LC1752.R58 2008
374.1826'942—dc22 2007052554

To my family,
and to the women
of Project Hope.

Contents

More Programs for The Children
Is There any one who really cares

Acknowledgments

Many people have made this book possible. First, I wish to express my deepest thanks to the teachers, staff, and learners of Project Hope who graciously shared their lives with me. This book is theirs as much as it is mine.

I am grateful to the professors at Northeastern University who inspired me when I was a doctoral student: Michael Brown, Christine Gailey, Ronald McAllister, Felix Padilla, Thomas Shapiro, and Lynn Stephen. I especially wish to thank my dissertation advisors Terry Haywoode, Wilfred Holton, and Gordana Rabrenovic.

I sincerely appreciate the support I have received from my colleagues at the University of Massachusetts-Boston's College of Public and Community Service (CPCS). There are many people to thank, especially Joan Arches, Luis Aponte-Pares, Shoshanna Ehrlich, Marie Kennedy, Andrew Leong, Terry McLarney, Sylvia Mignon, Jim O'Brien, Amelia Onorato, Andrés Paniagua, Ismael Ramírez-Soto, Margaret Rhodes, Deborah Schwartz, Vicky Steinitz, Michael Stone, Miren Uriarte, Ann Withorn, and Raul Ybarra. I wish to express a very special thanks to CPCS administrators and staff who made my work easier, in particular Sarah Bartlett, Margaret Eng, Linda Hardenbergh, Vanessa Cluny Louis, Shannon Nelson, Elaine Ward, Andrea Wight, and Evelyn Wong. I also appreciate the support I received from UMass colleagues Gissell Abreu-Rodriguez, Chris Bobel, Jean Humez, Nicole Lavan, Emmett Schaefer, Ester Shapiro, and Shirley Tang.

I am fortunate to have learned about ABE policies and practices from many wise colleagues at the Adult Literacy Resource Institute, the Boston Adult Literacy Fund, the Massachusetts Coalition for Adult Education, Systems for Adult Basic Education (SABES), WE LEARN, and World Education. I am especially grateful to Joanne Arnaud, Aliza Belzer, Sondra Cuban, Marcia Hohn, Jenny Horsman, Silja Kallenbach, Andy Nash, Steve Reuys, Klaudia Rivera, and David Rosen.

I owe a very special thanks to my hard-working, outstanding research assistants and to other students who helped me: Maria Christina Blanco, Joanne Callis, Valerie Flaherty, Jonathan Glancy, Jamie Lee Manning, and Cheryl-Ann Pizza-Zeoli (and Cathleen Higgins for use of her computer printer!). I am inspired by former students who work as teachers and advocates in adult education: Ernest Best, Keila DeOliveira, Meghan Doran, Cheryl Monahan, and Melaku Zewde.

I am most grateful for funding support from the Little Sisters of the Assumption NYC, the National Academy of Education's Postdoctoral Fellowship, Northeastern University, the Society for the Study of Social Problems' Racial and Ethnic Minority Scholarship, the Spencer Foundation's Dissertation Fellowship, and the University of Massachusetts-Boston Faculty Scholarship Grant. These grants made it possible for me to do extensive ethnographic fieldwork between 1995 and 2005. I would also like to thank my excellent editor, Rebecca Steinitz, and the editorial staff at the University of Illinois Press, especially Laurie Matheson.

This book would not have been possible without the love, encouragement, and support of my friends: Elizabeth Bettenhausen, Char Caver, Noel Doyle, Shobha Hamal-Gurung, Robert Hayden, Mike Leonard, Margaret McPartland, Mev Miller, Idelma Quintana, Anna Yangco, and the Brown family: Lenny, Jill, and Susan. I also wish to honor the memory of friends who passed away during the course of this research: Mary Chatman, Cathi Murray, Elizabeth Morrish, and especially, "Nana" Elsie Cohen.

Finally, I am indebted to my family: my loving parents, Aida and Paco, my beautiful sisters, Lety and Yvette, and my fabulous in-laws Richelle, Steve, and Todd. I also value the support I have received from my many cousins, aunts, and uncles in Chicago and Puerto Rico. I am truly blessed to have a wonderful family. Gracias a todos!

Most of all, I want to thank my partner and best friend, Keith Saunders, for patiently helping me realize my goals, making me laugh, and always believing in me.

List of Abbreviations

ABCD	Action for Boston Community Development
ABE	Adult Basic Education
AELS	Adult Education Literacy System
AFDC	Aid to Families with Dependent Children
ALP	Adult Learners Program
ALRI	Adult Literacy Resource Institute
CAAL	Council for Advancement of Adult Literacy
DOE	Department of Education
DSNI	Dudley Street Neighborhood Initiative
DSS	Department of Social Services
DTA	Department of Transitional Assistance
DYS	Department of Youth Services
ESOL	English for Speakers of Other Languages
GED	General Education Diploma
MCAS	Massachusetts Comprehensive Assessment System
NCLB	No Child Left Behind Act
NCSALL	National Center for Study of Adult Literacy and Learning
NIFL	National Institute for Literacy
TAFDC	Transitional Aid to Families with Dependent Children
TANF	Transitional Assistance to Needy Families
TTWC	Transition to Work Collaborative
WIA	Workforce Investment Act

The Second Annual

Mother's March

Please join us in celebrating and honoring all mothers, especially those mothering in poverty

Friday, May 12th
11:30 a.m.

March begins at City Hall
1 City Hall Square, Boston
Drinks provided • Bring your own lunch

For more information contact:
Coalition for Basic Human Needs • 617-497-0126

Introduction

> I feel that everybody should be treated equally, but in this society, that's not what happens. The rich get richer; the poor get poorer. The more we try to grow, the more they take from us. You know? Everything is on a time-limit. How can you put a time-limit when it's life?
>
> —Pam

I first visited the Adult Learners Program (ALP) at Project Hope, a family shelter located in one of Boston's poorest neighborhoods, in October 1995 with a group of professors from Northeastern University. The purpose of our visit was to develop community service opportunities for Northeastern students. After our meeting, I had a conversation with Lois O'Callahan, the coordinator of the ALP, who told me she was worried about proposed changes in Massachusetts's social welfare policies and their negative impact on the low-income families at Project Hope. O'Callahan discussed the misconceptions that were fueling the welfare reform debates, especially among welfare recipients themselves. Because I was teaching a class about social welfare at Northeastern, I volunteered to facilitate workshops about the new legislation and poverty-related issues. I also had a personal interest in learning more about the women who participated in Project Hope's programs. As the daughter of Puerto Rican immigrants, I benefited from social welfare programs throughout my childhood. My older sister, who dropped out of high school and later obtained her General Education Diploma (GED), experienced many of the challenges faced by the Project Hope women, such as homelessness and domestic violence. I saw the positive impact my sister's return to school had on her life, so I was inspired to learn more about women such as her. That initial visit became the impetus for a ten-year study of fifty homeless and formerly homeless mothers involved in the Adult Learners Program.

Each of the native-born women who attended classes at Project Hope lacked a high school diploma, and a number of the immigrant women had no formal schooling. Yet, I was immediately impressed by their positive attitudes and their determined belief in the life-changing power of education. Delila's desire to return to school was all-consuming: "I was so desperate. It's like you have an addiction or something. You know, how much you want it? If you don't get it, you're gonna die? That's how I felt about school." Other women were more pragmatic. Elizabeth, who obtained her GED in 1998, told me she enrolled in the ALP because, "I wasn't able to get a job, 'cause I didn't have a GED or high school diploma." Much research about why adults return to school confirms the importance of the GED to future job and education goals (Beder and Valentine, 1990; Fingeret and Drennon, 1997). Such as many of her peers, Renata's motivation was her children: "I decided to go back to school so I could be a good role model for my kids. Because how can I teach them something, or tell them something I don't know? How can I tell my kids to go to or finish school if I didn't?" As I listened to these women's stories, I wanted to know more about their previous schooling experiences. What poverty-related barriers interfered with their early schooling, and how did these barriers continue to pose obstacles to their participation in adult literacy classes? What social forces had limited their potential? What are the connections between education and social welfare policies?

The Project Hope women faced many personal and social barriers to participating in adult literacy education (for example, family violence), and welfare reform policies added another layer of obstacles to their quest for education. The women in the Adult Learners Program sought their goal of achieving a high school diploma within the context of homelessness and punitive welfare reform in the United States. In 1996, Massachusetts's welfare reform law imposed a "work-first" policy: welfare recipients were forced to forgo education and find employment as soon as possible. I observed welfare caseworkers advising women against enrolling in school because it would take "too long," and even though a number could pursue their GEDs, they still dropped out in a state of panic. Pam described her frustration with her caseworker:

> Yeah, the welfare system is real bad. They just want you to quit school right now and do volunteer work. I went to talk to the lady, and you

> know what she said? She said, "You have to do school on your own time! Because I am giving you sixty days to get a job, or sixty days to do volunteer work. And, we don't care if you go to school. That's what you are going to do on your time, when you have your free time. But you are going to do that volunteer work for us." When they told me this, I told Sister Lois [the ALP director]. I called her, I was crying on the phone, I was telling her that they wanted me to quit school. And I didn't want to. I want to finish. You know this is my second try. And last time it was hard because I had a baby. I went to LearningWorks downtown, but some nights I didn't have a babysitter, some nights the baby was sick, and I was scared, because my mother don't know about asthma. I had it rough!

The experience of Soledad, a formerly homeless, thirty-four-year-old Puerto Rican mother of four, embodies many of the struggles faced by the Project Hope women. In May 1996, I arrived at Soledad's third-floor apartment and found her taking care of ten children, four of her own plus six nieces and nephews. While Soledad spoke to the children in a bedroom where they were playing videogames, I sat in her living room, where I noticed a certificate of achievement prominently displayed on the wall. I remembered when Soledad received the award from the teachers in the ALP. She was honored for her hard work and improved literacy skills, but three months later she dropped out. Her welfare benefits were terminated because she had been "sanctioned" for not submitting Employment Services paperwork that documented her attendance in school and community service, and she had not filed an appeal in time. Soledad was frequently absent from school because she did not have reliable, affordable child care for her eighteen-month-old daughter, Neca. She had struggled with the Department of Transitional Assistance (DTA) for many years, constantly having to prove she needed public assistance for her four children. DTA told her she needed to find a job right away, but they would not approve a subsidized child care voucher until she actually obtained employment. Of course, Soledad could not go to job interviews without the child care voucher. To make matters worse, Soledad is severely learning disabled as a result of head injuries inflicted by her boyfriend in 1989. According to her medical records, she was hospitalized for severe head trauma and experienced memory loss as a result of the physical attack. To this day, she struggles with short-term memory loss, depression, anxiety, and posttraumatic stress.

Soledad told me her fifteen-year-old son needed ear surgery, her incarcerated boyfriend was up for parole in two weeks, and she was having trouble adjusting to the new antidepressants her doctor had recently prescribed. She was nervous and worried about how her life would change when her boyfriend was released from prison. At the same time, she hoped he would help her with child care so she could return to GED classes at Project Hope. (This did not happen because his parole officer pressured him to find employment as soon as possible.) Soledad sobbed as she told me how much she missed going to school every day, and how badly she wanted her high school diploma. She was also feeling isolated, and missed the sense of community and friendships that the ALP offered. When I left that day, I was struck by how much Soledad loved school, and by her passionate belief that the GED would solve her problems.

Soledad's strong desire to continue her education was shared by each of the women I met at Project Hope. Yet, throughout Boston, in 1996 and 1997, adult education classes funded by the Department of Transitional Assistance were cut, especially the classes for beginning students (Reuys, 1997). New time limits and strict attendance requirements further limited access. A study by the Adult Literacy Resource Institute suggests that the new policies purposefully reframed education programs to serve those who needed them least:

> Potential students may be looking at these time limits and deciding there's no point in starting to attend class since they wouldn't be likely to make enough progress in the time allowed. These two restrictions—on levels and on length of time—are part of an obviously intentional policy of "creaming"—that is, of serving only those people whose skills are initially rather good and who stand the best chance of being placed in a job within a year. The state has essentially ruled out education as an option for those whose abilities are lower and who are in fact in greatest need of further education. (Reuys, 1997, p. 2)

Yvette completed her GED in 1996, but did not join a building-trades program because the apprenticeship would take more than two years, and she was worried that it would jeopardize her future, rather than securing it: "I want something that's gonna be shorter so it won't put a stop on my plans, you know? Because if I start going to school and go into something that's gonna take three or four years, like they said, if you're absent three times they're gonna kick you out. . . . I mean, I think about all those things because I don't want to get out of the welfare and join them, and end up being kicked out because I was late, or something like that." Yvette's response points to the effect of the policies the Adult Literacy Resource Institute study described.

Several studies have documented significant dropout rates and declining enrollments in adult education in the aftermath of welfare reform

(D'Amico, 1998; Hayes, 1999; Imel, 2000; Kates, 1999; Knell, 1997; Pachikara, 1998; Sparks, 1999). Many of the adult education programs that had the greatest declines in enrollment were intensive (twenty hours a week), community-based programs that offered classes during the morning hours to accommodate the schedules of mothers with school-aged children (Reuys, 1997; Rivera, 1999a; Sparks, 1999). A number of these were popular education programs such as Project Hope's that, in addition to providing literacy instruction, were also aimed at fostering political empowerment and social change. Education for women such as those at Project Hope was clearly not a priority in welfare reform.

Welfare to What?

Kates (1999) sums up the problematic nature of welfare reform's stance toward education: "there is a disconnect between a) economic trends that indicate education and training levels of workers should be raised, and b) public assistance policies that have greatly reduced access to education and training for hundreds of thousands of women who are entering the workforce" (p. 1). According to D'Amico (2004), "Data from the 1992 National Adult Literacy Survey indicate a close relationship between low literacy and dependence on public assistance . . . the likelihood of being on welfare goes up as literacy levels go down; the two are intertwined (p. 21).[1] Indeed, increasing access to postsecondary education is essential to enhancing low-income women's socioeconomic opportunities; Kates (2004) is specific about the economic consequences: "Postsecondary education is necessary if women are to achieve earnings of $12 to $15 an hour" (p. 23). Nonetheless, in recent congressional hearings for the Committee on Education and the Workforce, New York University professor Lawrence Mead argued against a Senate bill that "would allow longer educational programs" for welfare recipients. He testified: "This would be a mistake. It would take welfare work policy back toward the era of the Family Support Act and JOBS when most recipients were allowed to substitute school or training for actual employment. . . . To allow recipients to turn welfare into a college scholarship also offends equity, since many taxpayers who pay for welfare lack the same opportunity. On both grounds, TANF should continue to stress work first" (p. 10).

Despite Mead's emphasis on work, however, work is neither the sole outcome of leaving welfare nor a guarantee of economic success. Since the passage of the 1996 Personal Responsibility and Work Opportunity Act welfare reform law, more than two million families and more than seven million individuals have left the welfare rolls; about

60 percent of those leaving Transitional Assistance for Needy Families (TANF) have transitioned to employment (United States Senate Committee on Finance, 2005, p. 2). However, according to Hays (2003), half of those employed remain in poverty, and we know little about the 40 percent of families that no longer receive public assistance and are not working. Welfare reform has been called a success because the numbers of welfare recipients who left the rolls defines success, and it does not matter if these families are still living in poverty. Kates (2004) critiques the many welfare "leaver" studies, finding that "higher wages were due to working more hours" and not higher earnings (p. 32). Kates shows how these welfare leaver studies measure success by numbers "off the rolls" and presents evidence that administrative sanctions (such as those placed on Soledad) also increased the numbers leaving welfare.[2]

One thing that is clear is that welfare policies continue to de-emphasize education (Polakow, 2004; Shaw et al., 2006). On June 28, 2006, Congress voted to reauthorize the Temporary Assistance for Needy Families program through September 2010 (Center for Budget and Policy Priorities, 2006). The Senate bill, the S667 Personal Responsibility and Individual Development for Everyone (PRIDE) Act, increases mandated work to thirty-four hours and allows rehabilitation services for substance abuse and other education activities to count toward work for up to six months. The House version of the bill (HR 240) is more conservative than the Senate's. It would require adult recipients to work forty hours a week instead of the current thirty hours. The bill reduces from one year to three months the amount of time that a person can count education and training as a direct work activity. It allows only three months of full-time adult education in any twenty-four-month period.

Punitive welfare reform legislation poses a contradiction: education is generally held to be the primary means of social mobility, but those who lack a high school diploma are expected to work in "any job," which typically means low-paying, service-sector jobs that will never lift them out of poverty. The 1996 punitive welfare law was popular with the general public because it was shaped by longstanding stereotypes about the causes of poverty and the belief that people are poor because there is something wrong with them as individuals (Abramovitz, 1996; Dujon and Withorn, 1996; Polakow, 1993). Polakow (1993) argues that the majority of people see poverty as a "private affair" whose "causes are rooted in failed individuals, failed families, and moral degeneration rather than in a failed public economy and a discriminatory public policy. It is an individual or underclass or ethnic problem in need of redress, not a structural one requiring a fundamental shift in our ways of seeing the politics of distribution" (p. 46). The ideology of neoliberalism has built upon these stereotypes to shape current policies on adult literacy education and welfare reform. According to Lyon-Callo (2004), "Neoliberalism is an embracing of privatization, marketization, and deregulation . . . it is more than just a set of practices and policies. Rather, it is a set of ideas and ways of imagining the world" (p. 11). Bloch, et al. (2003) argue that "The new discourses associated with neoliberalism relate the 'free market' and 'democracy' with discourses of autonomy, independence, flexibility, choice. Those demographically targeted as 'poor' or 'under the poverty line' are also 'dependents' who need through employment, to become independent and responsible" (p. 12).

Welfare-to-work programs typically operate on the false assumption that welfare recipients are irresponsible and do not work because they lack motivation and other "incentives." In fact, the majority of welfare recipients do work, often circulating between low-paying, unstable jobs, welfare, and the informal economy (Pachikara, 1998). All of the Project Hope women hated being on welfare because they felt dehumanized and stripped of their dignity, made to feel like there was something personally wrong with them. But my research at Project Hope, along with many other studies, shows that welfare-to-work programs do not lift people out of poverty. Welfare recipients with low literacy levels are pushed further into poverty when they are forced into low-paying jobs and denied access to education (D'Amico, 1998).

The Nature of Literacy and the Purpose of Education

D'Amico (1998) argues that the adult education field is currently being driven by welfare reform and its practices have become "impoverished by flawed assumptions about the relationships among literacy, poverty, education and work. . . . [T]he purpose of education is being increasingly defined as quick job placement" (p. 12). Though the question of how to define literacy and basic education has been copiously addressed, the answers are inevitably ideological. Quigley (1997) suggests there are "absolute standard definitions that use a grade-level set of skill criteria" and "relativist school" definitions that see literacy in context and "in relation to the cultural setting" (p. 13). Gee (1986) and others stress the "social context" of literacy and argue that literacy is "a cultural activity, reflecting a web of social expectations, beliefs, and accepted types of interaction with print" (quoted in Devine, 1994, p. 223). But according to the view that literacy is about "acquiring a set of skills," if students do not acquire or master the set of literacy "skills," then their failures are regarded as "personal," for literacy is constructed as "personal achievement" (Devine, 1994, p. 223).[3] We see here the connection to neoliberal ideologies.

In 1991, when Congress passed the National Literacy Act, it created the National Institute for Literacy (NIFL) and defined literacy as "an individual's ability to read, write, and speak in English, and compute and solve problems at levels of proficiency necessary to function on the job and in society, to achieve one's goals, and to develop one's knowledge and potential" (National Institute for Literacy, 1998). Under the proposed reauthorization of the 1998 Workforce Investment Act, the definition of literacy is changed to "an individual's ability to read, write, and speak in English, compute and solve problems proficiently." The omission from the language in the new bill of references to function in job or society, achieving one's goals, and developing one's potential points to the continued downgrading of the importance of education, especially for the uneducated, who are often the poorest.[4]

When the Project Hope women first enrolled in the ALP, they saw themselves as individuals and they did not trust other women. They talked about changing their "attitude" and needing to change from "within," before they were "ready to learn." They clearly had internalized the discourse of individual responsibility, believing that their life struggles owed to personal failures. A number of women said they were homeless because of their own "mistakes," and they blamed themselves for their poverty-related problems. The models of some drug rehabilitation programs reinforced individual responsibility by emphasizing "choices," as in the case of Billie, who said, "I choose to have a roof over my head, I choose not to be in the streets." In contrast to the sense of isolation and individual blame they brought to the program, however, she (and other women) learned how social forces limit their personal choices. This successful lesson—and the activism it inspired—was one of the many accomplishments of the ALP.

Laboring to Learn examines what happened to low-income women who participated in the ALP between 1995 and 2005. The popular education classes at Project Hope increased the women's senses of community, personal power, and social activism, and enabled them to break through the prejudices they held against themselves. The women came to understand how social forces impact their everyday lives and how their problems are linked to socioeconomic inequalities. They learned that the discourses regarding individual choice are woven into a hegemony that oppresses them. Mina described how she was transformed by her experience in the program because she learned to read and think critically about the world:

> When I first came here, I would not pick up a newspaper. . . . But after I came here, I didn't feel bad about picking up a paper, because I had a little understanding of why. I felt I could read. I could read my Bible now. But before, I was not reading or writing at all. You know? And it was like I was in a total dead world, living in a world not existing. And, you can't live in this world and not exist. Because I wasn't brought up to think. If you ain't brought up to think, you have a one-track mind, and whatever comes at you, that's what you accept.

But by 2000, many of the women were pressured to enroll in welfare-to-work training programs; they dropped out of adult literacy education to work in service-sector jobs at minimum wage. A number of women lost their welfare benefits and were transferred to other family shelters. Even the women who successfully completed their GEDs continued to struggle with homelessness, domestic violence, lack of child care, and other barriers to employment. Ultimately, Delila, Soledad, Pam, and the other participants in the ALP became entangled in a web of ideological contradictions regarding women's literacy within the context of social welfare reform in the United States. Benmayor, Torruellas, and Juarbe (1992) suggest that cultural stereotypes about poor women can be challenged by structural analyses that show how social and economic forces shape opportunities for people: "Arguing effectively against theories and explanations of cultural deficiency or behavioral deviance requires that research be more deeply grounded in people's lived experience. This type of inquiry takes a more careful look at the interplay between structural, cultural and symbolic factors with regard to life chances" (p. 13). It is my hope that *Laboring to Learn* offers such a framework for critical analysis of the impact of social policies and social inequalities on people's lives.

Chapter Overview

The next chapter, "Framing the Blame and Gain," discusses public discourses related to adult literacy, welfare reform, and poverty in the United States. How are the arguments for and against adult literacy education being "framed" within the context of social welfare reform? What is the logic behind "work-first" welfare reform? What are the prevailing myths about adult literacy? This chapter also examines how neoliberal discourses about individual choice, self-sufficiency, and personal responsibility shape the meaning and purpose of literacy within the context of social welfare reform. I suggest that welfare reform and neoliberal ideologies and practices have further compromised the democratic goals of critical literacy programs such as Project Hope's. What are the dominant "frames" that shape discourses about literacy—both historically and in today's global economy, when there is what some scholars call a decline of the "social state" (Rose, 1999)?

In chapter 2, "Hope on Magnolia Street," I describe the setting and context for this ethnographic study. Drawing upon archival data and interviews with staff and community activists, this chapter presents the history of Project Hope. The mission of Project Hope, founded in 1947 by radical Catholic nuns, is to confront and address the structural causes of homelessness. This chapter outlines the development of Project Hope's Adult Learners Program as well as community organizing efforts by Project Hope women in response to welfare reform.

Chapter 3, "Mothering in the War Years," draws upon in-depth interviews with Project Hope women to analyze the many poverty-related problems that affect the women's everyday lives. Some of these problems include: homelessness, lack of social supports and domestic violence. This chapter also examines the education histories of the women who participated in the ALP. The women describe how schools failed them, the social barriers they faced in school, how they value education, how they learn differently as adults, and their motivations to continue their education.

In chapter 4, "Around the Round Table," I present classroom portraits of the popular education classes at Project Hope. I describe the popular education approaches used by teachers in the Adult Learners Program, including how classes were based on the problems or "generative themes" in the lives of homeless women, and how teachers and learners developed "codes" to understand and solve these problems together. The chapter makes use of lesson plans and observations from Writing, Women and Society, Economic Literacy, Participatory Health Literacy, and "Loves Herself" community-building classes.

Chapter 5, "Women of Strength," is based upon follow-up interviews with the Project Hope women. The chapter also discusses ethnographic data from the Women's Economic Justice Project, the Women on the Rise workshops, and the video documentary, "Women of Strength: Stories from the Welfare Debate." It looks at the impact of the literacy program on the women learners, including how the women participated in social change activities, how they helped other women, how they increased their self-esteem, and how they advocated for their children's educations.

The concluding chapter, "Laboring to Learn, Learning to Labor," draws upon interviews with policymakers, researchers, and adult literacy teachers and practitioners to analyze what happened to the Project Hope women between 1995 and 2005. I present findings from a decade of research about welfare-to-work programs that show these programs alone do not help low-income women move out of poverty. I discuss the impact of welfare reform on adult literacy programs, and how the ABE system is serving as a weak safety net for those already "left behind" by poor schooling. This chapter ends with recommendations for supporting the education and social mobility of low-income mothers.

The Political Urgency of Adult Literacy Education

In *Laboring to Learn,* the voices of women learners, teachers, social service providers, community activists, and adult literacy practitioners present a compelling argument for increasing public funding for social welfare programs, as well as improving access to community-based adult literacy programs that serve low-income women. Much research shows that adults who lack basic literacy skills are at a serious social disadvantage, particularly with regard to securing quality employment opportunities and attaining social mobility (Carnevale and Desrochers, 1998; Holzer, 1996; Hunter and Harmon, 1979; Kozol, 1991; Quigley, 1997). The U.S. Department of Education reports that in the 1990s, enrollments in adult education were six times the enrollments in higher education, women participated in adult literacy education at higher rates than men, and African Americans and Latinos participated at higher rates than non-Hispanic whites in the most basic literacy classes (Kim, et al., 2004; National Center for Education Statistics, 2000).[5]

As U.S. states adopt educational reforms such as high-stakes testing, the failure of the elementary and secondary education systems to meet the needs of low-income and minority students are already being reflected in adult literacy education classes. Data on school dropouts and GED testing statistics suggest an increasing number of youth enrollments in adult secondary education programs (Hayes, 2000; Barton, 2005). According to the Council for the Advancement of Adult Literacy (CAAL) (2002), "Reform of the K–12 system, despite our best efforts and regardless of what it achieves, will leave an unacceptably large number of children behind" (p. 4). High-stakes testing may force the adult literacy education system to serve as an alternative for disadvantaged students (Comings, Sum, and Uvin, 2000). Now, more than ever, we must understand the relationship between educational reform and welfare reform. How do adult literacy education and social welfare policies intersect to limit education and economic opportunities for low-income women? Who (or what) is benefiting from these policies? Why do we continue to restrict educational opportunities for low-income women? In the chapters that follow, I seek to answer these questions.

1 *Framing the Blame and Gain*

> In practice neo-liberal policies involving market solutions may actually serve to reproduce—not subvert—traditional hierarchies of class and race, this should give us reason to pause.
>
> —Apple, 1999, p. 3

In his classic work, *Learning to Labor: How Working Class Kids Get Working Class Jobs* (1977), Paul Willis examines the purpose of schooling for a group of working-class boys in the U.K., showing how they "reproduced" themselves as members of the working class, how their ideologies and actions challenged authority figures, and how they created a "culture of resistance" within the context of public schooling. Willis's work sought to "blow the whistle" on the "contradictions and delusions" of the ideals and practices of liberal and social democratic education, as well as the role of the state in reforming public schools. Willis argues that

> Education seemed to offer the prospect of individualistic, humanistic development—the substance of the inalienable right to the pursuit of happiness—in relation to a promise for greater social equality (everyone was to be included in the possibility of advancement). The happy coincidence in all of this was that these joint aims—individual development and social equality—were compatible because they were also likely to make the economic system efficient anyway: there was a need for more skilled workers in the expanding and highly technological society. To give equality of opportunity was also to dredge the pool of talent amongst previously dispossessed groups. This would release new energies and skills needed by the expanding and technologically more advanced society. (p. 203)

In other words, when applied to disadvantaged people, the classic model of education inevitably links the individual's possibilities to his or her function in the economy—while masking that linkage under a discourse of equal opportunity.

Though Willis wrote *Learning to Labor* almost thirty years ago, his work provides much insight into why educational opportunities for American welfare recipients are increasingly limited. Willis argues that economic crises challenge the "compatibility between personal development and equality," for it is "plain to see that personal development leads to nowhere for some and to highly privileged positions for others . . . there is a world of difference between real equality in life, of expression and potential in all human beings, and mere equality of *opportunity*" [emphasis in original] (p. 204). The system, whatever its rhetoric, privileges some over others, and the privileged are often those who already have something going for them.

Apple (1999) studied the effects of globalization and neoliberalism on public education in the U.K., and argues that one of the effects of "market solutions" in public education is that schools have to show they are accountable, efficient, and productive, if they "wish to maintain or enhance their market position" (p. 8). Apple finds that marketized public school districts (including schools that had publicly funded vouchers, for example) engaged in "cream-skimming, ensuring that particular kinds of students with particular characteristics" are of greater value, producing better returns on the investment (p. 8). Apple's conclusions, more than twenty years later, support Willis's claims for the differentiating operations and effects of education.

Liberal and neoliberal educational practices raise important questions, including: What types of students are valuable in today's economy? Why and how is the public convinced that low-income women do not deserve the right to pursue a college education, or attain their high school diploma? How are the arguments for and against adult literacy education being "framed" within the context of social welfare reform? Why are women on welfare being forced into welfare-to-work programs? What is the logic behind "work-first" welfare reform? What are the prevailing myths about adult literacy? How do people with very low literacy skills fit into the global capitalist economy where "good" jobs require at least some postsecondary education? These questions provide an important context for understanding the experiences of low-income women who participate in literacy programs such as Project Hope's Adult Learners Program. In this chapter, I explore their implications, seeking to explain why education is such a challenge for these women, how current educational practices and policies in fact limit their opportunities, and why it is so difficult to promote critical literacy programs that both challenge the system and empower their participants. But this chapter also suggests why programs such as Project Hope's are so important.

The adult education field in the United States has historically struggled with its intended purpose and marginalized status in the discourse about education (D'Amico, 1998; Heaney, 1996; Hull, 1997; Quigley, 1997; Sticht, 2002).[1] Adult literacy education has contradictory goals. On the one hand, literacy is promoted as "good for the economy" because larger numbers of highly skilled workers generate greater productivity and profits, which in turn create more jobs. This uplifting goal appeals particularly to the corporations, politicians, and philanthropists who fund adult literacy education. On the other hand, literacy is promoted because it is good for a person's self-esteem, well-being, and family life. In this conception, literacy is good for society and fosters democracy: knowing how to read and write increases people's awareness of social problems and issues, and helps them navigate complex social systems. Though these may all seem like noble purposes, in the post-welfare era they are contradictory. In fact, people with low literacy skills are the cheapest sources of labor, and welfare-to-work subsidies for businesses that employ welfare recipients make "work-first" welfare reform profitable. Work-first welfare reform policies are intended to control the attitudes and behaviors of poor women. In today's economy, within the context of welfare reform, poor women are laboring to learn and learning to labor. Meanwhile, democracy is falling by the wayside.

The Politics of Literacy

In the sociology of education literature, the mainstream theories about literacy and education focus on the functions and responsibilities of schools in teaching basic literacy skills needed for the labor force, and on the role of schools in developing patriotic and productive citizens. The emergence of mass public education coincided with increasing industrialization and periods of high immigration to the United States in the mid 1800s. Public education became the means to teach immigrants and their children about American culture. Social historian Katz (1995) suggests that nineteenth-century American racism and fear of foreigners was the impetus for "cementing nativism to public schooling," and schools forced the assimilation of American culture on thousands of immigrants who were viewed as "shiftless," "ignorant," and criminal by the dominant political and social forces, especially the emerging Protestant middle class (p. 105).

The increasing industrialization of American society created a need for an educated workforce that possessed basic literacy skills: for example, people needed to read schedules and other directives. But schools also took on the role of teaching future workers the values of "work" under capitalism: "Institutions reflected the drive toward order, rationality, discipline, and specialization inherent in capitalism" (Katz, 1995, p. 107). The sociocultural evolution from an agricultural to a manufacturing economy had dramatic effects on the family and other social institutions. Whereas in agricultural societies work was organized according to changing seasons, customs, or traditions, in industrialized society it was now the responsibility of public schools to teach the values of "punctuality and time-driven labor" (Katz, 1995, p. 108).[2] Katz argues that another function of mass public education was to deal with the problem of changes in child labor laws and "idle youth": schools provided an important "day care" function for parents who worked. Given these economic imperatives, Katz observes, education for its own sake was hardly a priority: "A missing goal among the original purposes of public education [was] the cultivation and transmission of cognitive skills and intellectual abilities as ends in themselves. Public school systems existed to shape behavior and attitudes, alleviate social and family problems, and to improve poor people and reinforce a social structure under stress. The character of pupils assumed much more importance than their minds" (p. 110).

Bowles's and Gintis's *Schooling in Capitalist America* (1976) furthered the notion that the purpose of public schooling in capitalist economies is to produce workers who can meet the demands of a stratified labor market. Bowles and Gintis, as well as other so-called "reproduction" theorists (see Althusser, 1971; Bourdieu 1977) argue that schools actually reinforced social inequalities through their curriculum, pedagogy, and institutional relations. According to Aronowitz (1977):

> Schools reproduced the prevailing relations of production, including reproductive ideologies such as that of mobility, according to which those who failed to move up the class ladder were taught to blame themselves. After all, if society provides the opportunity to advance, but the individual does not succeed in either obtaining a credential needed to open doors of opportunity or, once having entered the corridors of power and mobility [does not succeed] in measuring up to standards, capitalism cannot be blamed. (p. x)

Following along these lines, in *Rethinking Literacy Education,* Quigley (1997) suggests that the history of literacy education is "located in social policies for regulation":

> The roots of literacy education in Britain and subsequently in America are located in social policies for regulation. From the beginning, literacy meant morality, and morality meant a safeguard against sin and unacceptable conduct . . . literacy education could bring a mode of conduct and way of life: habits, values, attitudes, which were based on the cultural necessities of progress and the requirements of society. . . . If adults, by dropping out of school or not attending at all, had not acquired the basics of literacy, literacy courses were provided, in large part to infuse morality for the good of the nation. The second chance was offered to certain adults by governments and educators and denied to others. (p. 74)

The rhetoric that adult literacy education provides a "second chance" continues to be popular among its mainstream supporters and practitioners. The image of adult literacy education as a "safety net" or "back-up" system to catch school failures is pervasive in the education literature. But though this image might seem to offer a positive framework for supporting those in need of education, it also generates the oppressive discourse about morality and personal irresponsibility that characterizes social constructions of the homeless person, the school dropout, the welfare recipient, and the illiterate—all poverty-related stigmas that apply to the Project Hope women (Goffman, 1986; Beder, 1991). "Illiterates" have been negatively depicted as society's scapegoats, their poverty linked to drug abuse, crime, low intelligence, poor work values, and other low-class behavior. One popular image of the "illiterate" according to Quigley (1997) is the adult learner as a "heroic victim," that is, "an innocent large child, who with nurturing, can be saved from the grip of illiteracy and its evils. The popular perspective creates a role for a rescuer" (1997, p. 25). Thompson's (1980) research examines the discourse in literacy policies and materials and finds "the language of personal deficit, affliction, and the need for treatment to rehabilitate the malfunctioning adult into normal society runs like a checklist through the literature" (quoted in Quigley, 1997, p. 38).

In these images, we see, as Quigley describes it, how society can both "despise and pity, fear and want to help at the same time" (p. 38). Understanding how literacy and illiteracy are socially constructed is important because these stereotypes serve particular power interests that are committed to maintaining a pool of bodies at the bottom of the social and economic ladder. These images also help explain why adult literacy education is marginalized in the popular discourse about public education and why its programs are especially vulnerable to budget cuts: the students who participate in them are typically school dropouts and immigrants, perceived as native failures and illegal aliens who, in difficult times, do not deserve taxpayers' support.

The Purposes of Education and Literacy

Adult literacy education in the United States dates back as early as the Revolutionary War. Over the years, literacy instruction has been offered by religious institutions, civic and charitable community groups, and the U.S. military, as well as via "vocational apprenticeships" (Sticht, 2002). But it became a focus of public policy in the early 1960s. According to Sticht (2002) there were four "critical social forces" that led to the public funding of the Adult Education Literacy System (AELS): "the role of the U.S. military, the movement for self-improvement and charitable activities, immigration, and the movement for a liberal education that makes good citizens versus human resource development for economic productivity" (p. 14). Demetrion (2005), Heaney (1996), Rose (1991), and Quigley (1997) have all studied the history of and political battles to fund adult literacy education in the United States. In 1962, the first adult literacy education bill was introduced in the House, but it quickly died in Congress. However, in that same year the Manpower Development and Training Act (MDTA) passed; it was more attractive because it highlighted the importance of basic reading and writing skills for effective participation in the workforce (Quigley, 1997). Two years later, President Johnson signed the historic Economic Opportunity Act of 1964 (Public Law 88-42): Title IIB created the Adult Basic Education Program; Title IA created Job Corps Training Centers (Quigley, 1997; Sticht, 2002). In 1965, the American Council on Education allowed Job Corps participants to take the General Education Diploma (originally developed for American soldiers and military personnel). As the GED was made available beyond the military, it became a major component of adult literacy education. In 1966, the Adult Education Act was passed as an amendment (Title III) to the Elementary and Secondary Education Act of 1965. This legislation placed adult basic education programs under the administration of the U.S. Office of Education (Quigley, 1997; Sticht, 2002).

In the 1970s and 80s an approach to literacy education that has been labeled "functional" literacy gained popularity throughout the United States. According to a definition offered by Hunter and Harmon in *Adult Illiteracy in the United States* (1979), functional literacy is: "The pos-

History of Adult Basic Education (ABE) in the United States

1930s	New Deal programs such as Civilian Conservation Corps and Works Progress Administration offer basic literacy instruction.
1932	Formation of the Highlander Folk School by popular educator, Myles Horton.
1942	General Educational Development (GED) Test developed for U.S. military services.
1962	First Adult Literacy Act introduced, but defeated.
1962	Manpower Training and Development Act and Area Redevelopment Act are passed.
1964	Adult Basic Education Act is adopted in Title IIB, Economic Opportunity Act (P.L. 88–452).
1965	GED testing becomes available to Job Corps trainees and other civilians.
1965	First federally funded ABE teacher training programs are developed.
1966	Adult Basic Education Act (AEA) is renewed, but transferred to U.S. Office of Education.
1968	Amendments to AEA allow for private nonprofits to be eligible for state grants.
1970s	Amendments to AEA change eligibility to define adults as those sixteen years or older; the purpose is expanded to those in need of secondary education; and funding for English language learners and bilingual ABE programs is provided.
1978	Amendments to AEA encourage delivery of services beyond schools, and a greater focus on basic literacy education and English language learners.
1980s	Amendments encourage use of volunteers, privatization of delivery systems (1984), new requirements for standardization of services, and accountability measures; expansion of workplace and English as a second language programs.
1991	National Literacy Act (P.L. 102–73) replaces AEA of 1966 and introduces new definition of literacy. The National Institute for Literacy is established.
1998	Workforce Investment Act (P.L. 105–220) Title II, The Adult Education and Family Literacy Act, replaces the National Literacy Act of 1991. WIA emphasizes workforce development.
2006	Workforce Investment Act is reauthorized as the Job Training Improvement Act. Faith-based providers and for-profit sectors are eligible for funding.

Note: "For the purposes of this Act the term *literacy* means an individual's ability to read, write, and speak in English, and to compute and solve problems at levels of proficiency necessary to function on the job and in society, to achieve one's goals and develop one's knowledge and potential" (quoted in Rose, 1991, p. 28).

Sources: Rose, 1991; Heaney, 1996; DeSanctis, 1979; Ellis, 1984; Sticht, 2002; Yoho, 2005.

session of skills *perceived as necessary by particular persons and groups* to fulfill their own self-determined objectives as family and community members, citizens, consumers, job-holders, and members of social, religious, or other associations of their own choosing" (emphasis in original, quoted in Brodkey, 1991, p. 162). In practice, however, the functional literacy perspective, as supported by United States policymakers, focuses on work-related objectives. Just as the first public schools in the mid 1800s were developed in response to the needs of the labor market and social problems related to industrialization, contemporary literacy campaigns continue to emphasize the acquisition of reading and numeracy skills in order to increase access to better jobs and increase economic productivity. This is evident in the 1998 National Institute for Literacy's *Literacy: It's A Whole New World* public awareness campaign: "Changing economic, demographic, and labor-market forces are creating a human capital and skills deficit that threatens U.S. competitiveness and acts as a barrier to individual opportunities for all Americans" (National Institute for Literacy, 1998; see also ProLiteracy Worldwide, 2006).

Human Capital Theory is an important theoretical framework for understanding the primacy of functional literacy in contemporary adult literacy education. According to Heaney (1996):

> Under the expanding influence of capitalism, Human Capital Theory became the dominant rationale for most public adult education—a theory which holds that long-term benefits or rate of return from an individual's investment in education are superior to other forms of investment. Learners became "human capital" and the function of adult education was instrumentally reduced to the development of human (as distinct from natural or technological) resources. . . . Adult education no longer emphasized reflection, but rather the diffusion of knowledge. Adult education, which was first conceived as a tool for social change, became a functional tool. It became an enterprise determined by the market, without clear social goals. (p. 15)

Beder (1987) similarly argues that: "Human Capital Theory has become the dominant rationale for all public subsidy of adult education including adult literacy, job training programs and to a large extent, even the Cooperative Extension Service. From a public policy perspective, the overriding purpose of adult education is to enhance economic productivity" (p. 109).

However, Human Capital Theory and economic rationales for literacy education do have their critics, who recognize that the failure to critically consider the causes and effects of poverty leads to the development of bad public policies that do not really address the root causes of the problems but rather make them worse. Giroux (1981) argues that, "In spite of its appeal to economic mobility, functional literacy reduces the concept of literacy and the pedagogy in which it is suited to the pragmatic requirements of capital; consequently, the notions of critical thinking, culture and power disappear under imperatives of the labour process and the need for capital accumulation" (quoted in Macedo, 1991, p. 151). Demetrion (2005) criticizes the view that adult literacy education can lead to "employment, self-sufficiency, and general life enhancement" and argues that a "literacy myth" guides current policies (p. 215; see also: Corley, 2003; Auerbach, 1992). According to Demetrion (2005), "sufficient jobs for poorer, minority groups do not exist in sufficient numbers that pay sufficiently well to create pathways out of poverty" (p. 215). Auerbach (1992) puts the point directly: "The literacy myth serves an ideological function that masks the gap between the poor and other groups, which perpetuates the fable of equality, hence, the viability of democracy itself, as it pertains to social and economic opportunity" (quoted in Demetrion, 2005, p. 215).

Furthermore, Shaw, et al. (2006) argue that the federal work-first ideology has "decoupled" education from work and poses contradictions to human capital models. Shaw, et al. highlight contradictory ideology, in both welfare reform and the Workforce Investment Act, that has "usurped human-capital ideals" (pp. 2–3) that traditionally linked education to work. They studied how "work-first" policies restrict welfare recipients' access to college education and argue that "evidence clearly indicates that welfare reform and WIA cemented a 'sea change' in national thinking about the role of education in the lives of poor people. Whereas education is commonly acknowledged to be a sure and consistent route to self-sufficiency, recent federal policy has effectively removed this pathway for our poorest citizens" (p. 3).

The Changing Economy

> Only a generation ago, adults with relatively low basic skills could earn a living and have a good life if they were willing to work hard. This is no longer the case. Since 1980, the wage difference between adults without a high school diploma, those with a high school diploma, and those with post-secondary education has steadily grown wider. This trend helps explain why the current income differential between the top 20 percent and the bottom 20 percent is at a historic high. In 1997, high school graduates earned an average of 42 percent more than those with less than a high school education, and this wage gap continues to grow (National Institute for Literacy, 2000, p. 7).

Economic conditions in the last several decades disprove the myth of equal opportunity. Since the early 1970s, economic inequality in the United States has increased dramatically. Economist Levy (1987) studied income statistics as a framework for understanding economic changes since World War II. He argues that between 1947 and 1973 there was steady income growth among Americans, but by 1975 this growth ended; income inequality today is as great as it was at the end of World War II (pp. 12–22). Several factors have been advanced as explanations for this change. For example, Freeman (1993) suggests that one contributing factor is the decline in union membership in the United States, which, in his view, led to lower wages and increasing inequality. Albelda and Tilly (1997) argue that government policies such as tax benefits for businesses and increased taxes for the working and middle classes also increased economic inequality. In addition, government support for social welfare programs decreased, especially during the Reagan administration (Abramovitz, 1996; Dujon and Withorn, 1996). Harrison and Bluestone (1988) highlight changes in the nature of the labor market in the United States: "[T]he nation is producing jobs by the bushel, but corporate restructuring, aided and abetted by permissive government policy, is producing a startling deterioration in the quality of those jobs and consequently in the standard of living of a growing proportion of our citizens" (1988, p. 113). They note that the shifts from the higher-paying manufacturing sector to the lower-paying, less stable service sector constitute a major reason that wages in the United States have declined since 1973. Globalization has also contributed to declining economic opportunities for Americans (Castells, 2000; Project South, 2002; Hallgren and Weiner, 2003).[3]

The labor market outlook in Massachusetts is consistent with these national trends. Massachusetts lost about two hundred thousand jobs between 2001 and 2003 (Bushnell, 2006). According to the Massachusetts Budget and Policy Center in 2004, "Massachusetts has witnessed one of the sharpest drops in employment in the country over the past several years and long-term unemployment is now more prevalent here than nationally" (p. 1). Since September 2005, the Massachusetts Department of Workforce Development reports a modest 1 percent gain in job growth, which is the strongest gain in employment since the end of 2003 (Bushnell, 2006); as of July 21, 2006, the Massachusetts Department of Workforce Development reported that the state's unemployment rate "held steady" at 5 percent (Gavin, 2006, p. 1). The majority of new jobs in Massachusetts are at the ends of the employment spectrum: in high-paying sectors such as technology, education, and health services, and in the low-paying retail services sector (Massachusetts Budget and Policy Center, 2004).[4] Not surprisingly, younger workers, workers with a high school education or less, and African American and Latino workers all experience higher rates of unemployment. There are also "considerable inequities" between men's and women's earnings (Massachusetts Budget and Policy Center, 2006; Massachusetts Budget and Policy Center, 2004). The employment outlook is thus particularly bleak for low-income, undereducated women of color such as the Project Hope women. Without an education that goes significantly beyond functional literacy, they have little hope of truly transforming their circumstances, let alone transforming the social and economic conditions that create and maintain those circumstances.

The Declining Social State of Governing

In the introduction, I discussed the current dominance of neoliberal ideologies that also directly affect the lives of women such as the Project Hope women. These discourses not only have changed social policies, but have led to what some scholars are calling a decline in the "social state" (Rose, 1999). "In place of the social state that tried to legislate the care of citizens, the nonsocial state is a new way to govern through the flow of ideas and knowledge that construct new cultural ways of thinking about ourselves as well as others and their care. While the social state was developed to take care of citizens, abstractly, in postindustrial 'knowledge' and 'networked' societies, now local communities and individuals take care of each other" (Bloch, et al., 2003, p. 21). Previous iterations of the social state "help[ed] citizens learn how to take care of themselves as well as others, and to socially administer, the freedom of self and other [via] state welfare policies and practices of salvation and intervention" (Bloch, et al., 2003, p. 14). But today, neoliberalism offers "both a return to classic liberalism's embracing of the private, 'free' market as the solution to social problems and an embracing of the role of government to promote individualized competition and market-based policies" (Lyon-Callo, 2004, p. 10).

Lyon-Callo's (2004) ethnographic study of staff, administrators, and advocates working at a homeless shelter supports his contention that a "hypothesis of individualized deviancy is at the root of contemporary responses to homelessness" (p. 12). Lyon-Callo illustrates the growing trend to privatize social services for the homeless, services that primarily focus on mental health, physical health, substance abuse, and privatized job training—that is, on the individual rather than the society. Yet, he argues, as "the failure of the continuum of care to decrease homelessness should make clear by now, the problems causing homelessness lie not so much in how services are delivered, but rather in what services do and do not do" (p. 12). Current services are based firmly upon neoliberal ideologies:

> [P]eople are now governed through their commitments to particular communities of morality and identity. . . . Rather than being governed by others, people are now encouraged to govern themselves as 'responsible' or 'contributing' community members if they wish to receive any material or social benefits. . . . There is no guarantee of any degree of social welfare or social well-being for those failing in their responsibility as community members. (Lyon-Callo, 2004, p. 110)

Indeed, rhetoric about "self-sufficiency" runs rampant throughout proposals to reform social welfare programs (including public housing). Bratt and Keyes (1997) studied how nonprofit housing organizations "think about and promote self-sufficiency for their residents" (p. 1). Their study included Project Hope, and they interviewed Sister Margaret Leonard, Project Hope's executive director. According to Bratt and Keyes, the concept of "family self-sufficiency" was "formalized" by the federal government in the National Affordable Housing Act of 1990:

> Self-sufficiency has become an increasingly important goal as the federal government has articulated its growing dissatisfaction with programs it perceives as fostering long-term dependency. The 1996 welfare reform legislation, although a clear effort to reduce net expenditures, also has a powerful ideological message, which apparently enjoys bipartisan support: Traditional assistance programs have undermined and worked against the goal of economic independence. (p. 1)

However, the researchers found "objections to the term self-sufficiency" because "it evokes an image of rugged individualism, which is no more or less applicable to low-income people than it is to the rest of society. 'Self-sufficiency' implies that people who participate in such programs will, at some point, no longer need any outside supports and, instead, will be totally able to care for themselves. In contrast, it can be argued that no one in our society is truly self-sufficient" (Bratt and Keyes, 1997, p. 9). They also note that a number of the participants in their study suggested that the term self-sufficiency had a "negative connotation," because "until you achieve 'self-sufficiency,' you are somehow 'insufficient'" (p. 9).

Apple (1999) argues that "in classical liberalism the individual is characterized as having an autonomous human nature and can practice freedom. In neoliberalism the state seeks to create an individual who is an enterprising and competitive entrepreneur" (Apple, 1999, p. 5). Apple adds:

> It is not that the conception of the self-interested subject is replaced or done away with by the new ideals of Neoliberalism, but that in an age

> of universal welfare, the perceived possibilities of slothful indolence create necessities for new forms of vigilance, surveillance, performance appraisal and of forms of control generally. In this model the state has taken it upon itself to keep us all up to the mark. The state will see to it that each one makes a continual enterprise of ourselves in what seems to be a process of governing without governing. (p. 5; also see Olsen, 1996, p. 340)

Under these new governing patterns one can no longer expect the state to take care of its citizens, to provide for their basic human needs such as shelter and food, nor are citizens entitled to publicly funded healthcare or education. All citizens must be self-sufficient and personally responsible for their life circumstances. Yet current literacy programs and policies hardly provide the education and support that people might need to achieve these goals; indeed, this very rhetoric leads them to fail.

Framing the Blame

The recent history of welfare reform in Massachusetts encapsulates many of the issues discussed so far in this chapter and points to the power of stereotypes. In 1994, when Clarabel Ventura, a twenty-six-year-old mother of six, was arrested for abusing her four-year-old son, her disturbing case fueled the drive to reform welfare in Massachusetts. The news broke that Ventura's mother, Eulalia, had received welfare benefits from 1969 to 1992, and four generations of Ventura's family—all seventeen of Eulalia's children, seventy-four grandchildren, and fifteen great-grandchildren—had received public assistance. For conservatives, Ventura was a "textbook case" for welfare reform, and pundits estimated that Ventura's extended family had cost taxpayers from $750,000 to $1 million a year (Sennott, 1994, p. 1). At the time, Joseph V. Gallant, commissioner of the Department of Public Welfare, suggested that Ventura was a "statistical aberration," but that "generational dependency" on welfare was becoming a norm. The Massachusetts Department of Public Welfare's records disputed the generational dependency assertion, but Commissioner Gallant said, "The fact is that the system allows this. The point is that this is what welfare has become; the pattern is to move from state welfare to federal programs. It has become cradle-to-grave funding for these families. That's why the system needs to be overhauled" (Sennott, 1994, p. 1). *Boston Globe* columnist Mike Barnicle (1994) pointed to the problematic discourse at the heart of the case: "Ventura has done for the welfare debate what Willie Horton accomplished for the prison furlough program, sent it crashing and burning to the basement where the mere mention of the woman's name—Claribel [*sic*]—immediately invokes the darker spirits within us: Everyone getting assistance is a dirty, rotten, fat, lazy, no-good minority fraud simply intent on breeding and scamming a check, all the while laughing at the rest of us who work hard to support them" (p. 33).

After heated battles in the state legislature, where Ventura's case was invoked over and over again, on February 10, 1995, Massachusetts governor William Weld signed into law comprehensive welfare reform legislation. The Department of Public Welfare's name was changed to the Department of Transitional Assistance (DTA), and the influence of neoliberal ideologies and poverty stereotypes are evident in the following documents prepared by DTA:

> The legislation provides benefits to support recipients who work and offers them an opportunity to move from a system that fostered dependency to one that promotes self-sufficiency. . . . This program offers hope and opportunity for parents and children to break the multi-generational link to a system that has, albeit unintentionally, stifled their economic and social maturation. It sounds an end to an approach that all too often victimized rather than helped families. (Commonwealth of Massachusetts Department of Transitional Assistance, 1995, p. 1)

As with the stereotypes about illiterates discussed earlier in this chapter— representations of infantilization and disease—immorality and dependence are pervasive in the literature about women on welfare. Americans continue to believe that welfare recipients are lazy and not motivated to work, but rather choose to be poor. A 1994 report published by the Heritage Foundation argued that "behavioral poverty was abundant and growing at an alarming pace [and] went on to define behavioral poverty as 'a cluster of severe social pathologies including: an eroded work ethic and dependency, the lack of educational aspirations and achievement, an inability or unwillingness to control one's children, as well as increased single parenthood, illegitimacy, criminal activity, and drug and alcohol use'" (Abramovitz, 1996, p. 20). This image of pathology serves to distance the poor from mainstream society; ironically, that distancing contributes to the difficulty poor people have in achieving mainstream success.

There is extensive critique regarding the social construction of the welfare recipient (Schram, 2000). In *Under Attack, Fighting Back: Women and Welfare in the U.S.* (1996), Abramovitz writes, "The misperceptions about welfare stem from the stereotyping of poor women and welfare; the systematic refusal of the media to cover ongoing resistance to harsh welfare reforms that have been organized by welfare mothers and their supporters around the country, and the bankrupt leadership of politicians who insist on playing to the worst instincts of the voters" (p. 10). Several histories of social welfare programs in the United States illustrate how welfare recipients have been society's scapegoats and used to "ease public concerns about other social, economic, and political issues; and to divert public attention from the true causes of the nation's woes" (Abramovitz, 1996, p. 11; see also: Katz, 1995; Gordon, 1990; Schram, 2000). Addressing these stereotypes, both with the women themselves and in the larger community, is one of the goals of Project Hope's Adult Learners Program.

Project Hope and an Alternative Vision of Adult Literacy Education

In subsequent chapters, I discuss at length the history, philosophy, and curriculum of Project Hope's Adult Learners Program. Here, though, it is essential to note that the literacy philosophy of the ALP is diametrically opposed to the economically based tenets of Human Capital Theory and functional literacy. Building on the work of Brazilian educator Paulo Freire and other theorists and practitioners of democratic adult literacy education, the teachers and learners at the ALP developed a literacy practice based on self-awareness and cultural critique as the foundation of literacy skills. In their vision, literacy is a means of enabling democratic participation in social change, as well as individual advancement; indeed, the structure of the program stresses the value of collective learning, as learners work together to achieve group and individual goals.

Yet almost from its beginnings, the ALP has operated in a hostile environment. Despite evidence of striking economic inequalities in American society, in 1996 President Clinton signed the Personal Responsibility and Work Opportunity Act, "ending welfare as we know it" and symbolically ending the government's responsibility to assist the poor. D'Amico (1998) convincingly argues that the adult education field has subsequently been driven by welfare reform, and its practices have become "impoverished by flawed assumptions about the relationships among literacy, poverty, education and work" (p. 12). Implicitly advocating for a perspective similar to Project Hope's, D'Amico suggests that "seeing literacy as part of a web of factors that influence the ability of individuals to support families by working, is not the same as assessing literacy programs by their ability to place individuals in jobs . . . the purpose of education is being increasingly defined as quick job placement" (p. 12). For D'Amico and many others, this is clearly a problem.

In 1998, the Workforce Investment Act (WIA) was passed and posed further challenges to the adult education field. The new law consolidated more than fifty employment, training, and literacy programs into three block grants to states (Commonwealth of Massachusetts Department of Education, 1999). Under Title II of the law, the Adult Education and Family Literacy Act was enacted to:

> 1) assist adults to become literate and obtain the knowledge and skills necessary for employment and self-sufficiency;
> 2) assist adults who are parents to obtain the educational skills necessary to become full partners in the education of their children; and
> 3) assist adults in the completion of a secondary school diploma. (Murphy, 2003, p. 3)[5]

The WIA requires a far greater degree of coordinated services between adult education and job training than in the past. For example, adult education programs funded by the state are required to work with their Regional Employment Boards (referred to as "One-Stop Career Centers"). The Adult Education and Family Literacy Act "mandated controversial new student performance measures for all federally funded programs and required all states to rewrite their adult education plans. The performance measures focused on job readiness rather than more holistic concerns, a fact that continues to outrage many people in the field" (Speights, 2001, p. 1). Sparks (1999, 2003) studied the impact of welfare policy on educational advocates and adult literacy practitioners and found that "education advocates are struggling over control for the meaning and definition of education for work" (Sparks, 2003, p. 2). She writes,

> There is a heterogeneous configuration of elements among and within advocate positions. As a result, those who work on behalf of welfare recipients, may in fact be working at cross purposes. . . . There are struggles over differences in ideologies between welfare reform's emphasis on job preparation versus the contested and contradictory ideologies of adult education for individual development or for social change; there are struggles over educational program goals and purposes causing major conflicts between welfare proponents and ABE practitioners; and there are ethical struggles silencing participant voices as well as ABE instructor voices where a politics of control is in play. (p. 3)

This book is itself an intervention in this struggle: it gives voice to learners and instructors in an adult literacy education program, and it makes a clear case for the limitations of the current dominant ideologies of welfare reform and functional literacy.

Conclusion

Throughout United States history, oppressed groups of people—slaves and their descendants, Native Americans, Mexican Americans, women—have been denied access to basic literacy and civil rights, which have often been entwined (Takaki, 1993; Zinn, 2003). In the 1880s the United States used literacy tests to restrict immigration and determine who could become an American citizen. Later, literacy tests were frequently used to restrict voting by African Americans. Today, the denial of literacy is a common practice in many American welfare offices, as low-income women on welfare, many of whom are school dropouts, are tracked into dead-end jobs and welfare-to-work programs that "train" them to be low-wage service workers.

Building upon Willis's (1977) work, in the following chapters of *Laboring to Learn* I further examine the "ideological messages" low-income women hold about welfare-to-work and literacy. Like Willis, I use ethnography to highlight contradictions in the schooling experiences of low-income women of color. Willis insists that "social reproduction and contradiction must be shown not as abstract entities, but as embedded dynamically within the real lives of real people" (p. 202). He argues that "the role of ethnography is to show the cultural viewpoint of the oppressed, their hidden knowledges and resistances as well as the basis on which entrapping decisions are taken with some sense of liberty, but which nevertheless help to produce structure" (p. 203). This is the goal of the remaining chapters in *Laboring to Learn.*

Like Willis's "lads," the formerly homeless "ladies" in the ALP internalize hegemonic ideas about their roles and responsibilities as individuals, especially with regard to being good mothers who take good care of their families and find employment. As well, the women believe in the liberal democratic ideal of public education as a means of social mobility—they strongly believe that a high school diploma will open doors of economic opportunity. Yet, the Project Hope women, as welfare recipients, also face the contradictory notion that they are not deserving of literacy or education, and that they are failures because they acted irresponsibly by dropping out or becoming homeless. Within the context of neoliberal ideologies and practices, the women are constructed as personally responsible for their poverty and for all of the problems they face in their lives.

In the next chapter, I contextualize this ethnographic study by describing the setting in which the Project Hope women learned. According to its mission statement, Project Hope is "Dedicated to building community that promotes dignity, self-reliance, and interdependence. We strive to be compassionate in creating new structures, which support families, and to be unyielding in challenging systems that threaten basic human rights. We know this stance to be one of struggle and joy" (Project Hope, 1984). In the pages that follow, I describe how Project Hope, its social services, and the Adult Learners Program were developed in response to the Dudley community's changing needs and the expressed desires of low-income women. Drawing upon interviews with staff, adult learners, and program directors, I present the voices of Project Hope women and staff who reflect on the history of Project Hope, the social services it offers, and the various advocacy initiatives that emerged as a result of Massachusetts's welfare reform. In so doing, I begin to show the real effect on real people of the theoretical issues this chapter has outlined.

2 *Hope on Magnolia Street*

> Poverty is not something that's created by individual families and it's not resolved by the empowerment of individual families. Community is absolutely critical and essential. And building the communal infrastructure for families, that has always been a part of our life.
>
> —Sister Margaret Leonard, executive director, Project Hope

The Dudley neighborhood where Project Hope is located is less than two miles from downtown Boston. It includes an area of about 1.3 square miles in northeastern Roxbury, with the South End to the north, and Dorchester to the east and south. When I first visited the Dudley neighborhood in 1993, it reminded me of the Humboldt Park neighborhood in Chicago where I grew up. There were several immigrant-owned small businesses on Dudley Street, Blue Hill Avenue, and Columbia Road, along with an abundance of liquor stores and bodegas, apartment buildings in need of repairs, and trash strewn on vacant lots and sidewalks. I loved hearing Puerto Rican women speaking Spanish when I rode the No. 15 bus from Dudley Station to Upham's Corner, watching the neighborhood youth play basketball at Hannon courts, and being shaken up by loud beats coming from a Toyota slowly cruising the street. All this, and the diversity of people who lived in the neighborhood, made me feel right at home.

Dudley is like many other urban neighborhoods that struggle with a variety of social problems related to structural inequalities, and that have experienced significant social and economic changes in the last century. In *Hope: 50 Years of the Little Sisters of the Assumption on Magnolia*

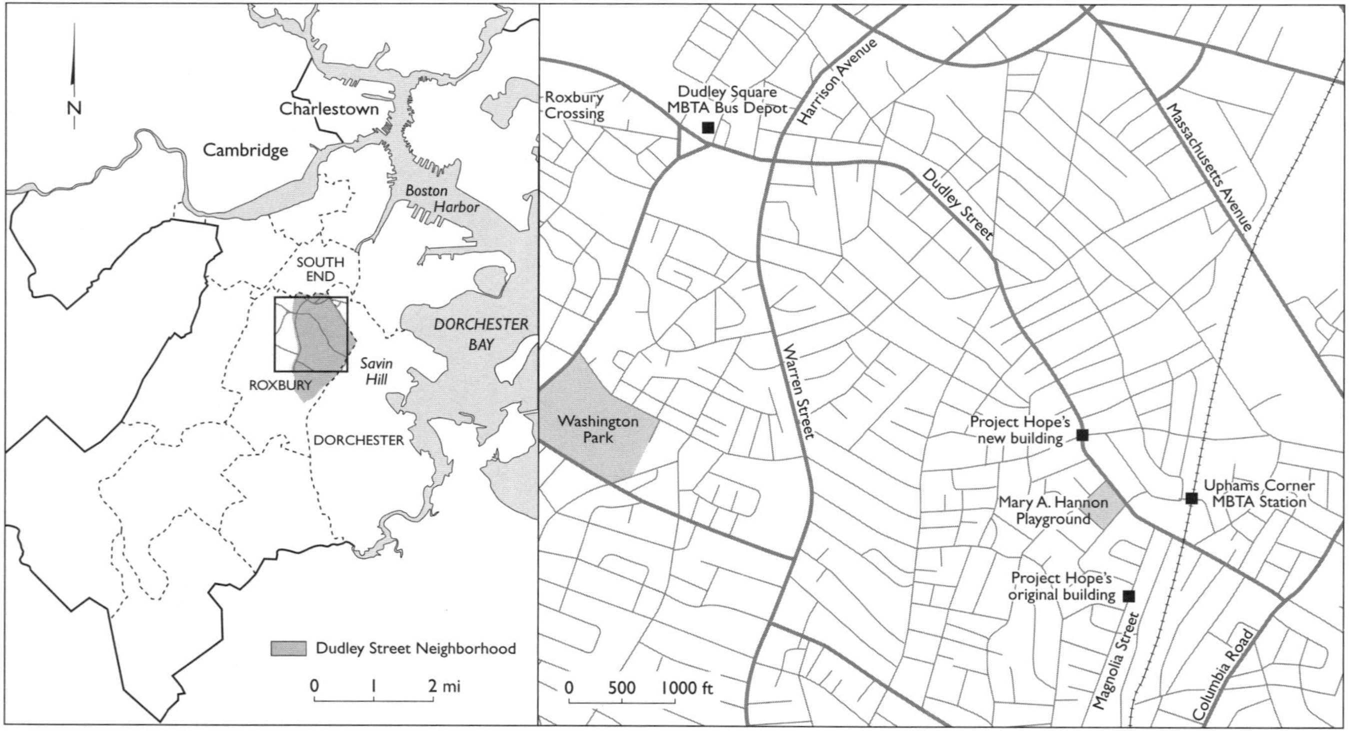

Map of Dudley neighborhood

Street in Dorchester (1997), Will Holton of Northeastern University describes the neighborhood's history:

> In the early 20th century, Dorchester and Roxbury were dominated by Irish-Americans while some Protestant families remained from the earlier period. Jewish families were coming into the area by the 1920s from the North End and West End, establishing a strong presence on Blue Hill Avenue. After World War II, large parts of Dorchester and Roxbury changed rapidly as many Irish and Jewish residents sought better housing and schools farther from the inner city and were replaced by African-Americans, mostly from the American south, who were seeking economic opportunity and less discrimination in the north. Many absentee landlords let their properties deteriorate badly and by the 1970s some of them burned their buildings for the insurance money. At the same time, the city turned its back on the needs of Dorchester and Roxbury. (p. 2)

Today, when compared with the city of Boston as a whole, the residents of the Dudley neighborhood are poorer and younger, and more ethnically diverse:

—Almost two-thirds of Dudley residents are under thirty-five years of age, and more than one-third of Dudley residents are under the age of nineteen (Dudley Street Neighborhood Initiative [DSNI], 2003)

—Half of all Dudley households are families with children under the age of eighteen (DSNI, 2003)

—Dudley has more single-parent and other nontraditional families (single adult heads of household living with kin other than their own children, such as grandparents) than does Boston overall (DSNI, 2003)

—In 2000, Dudley adults were less likely to have completed a bachelor's or graduate degree than their counterparts across the city (11 percent vs. 36 percent) and more likely not to have completed high school (35 percent vs. 21 percent) (Bacon, Russell, and Tighe, 2003, p. 16)

—In the Dudley area, 37 percent of the immigrants came to the United States in the last decade, compared to 48 percent in Boston overall (Bacon, Russell, and Tighe, 2003, p. 4)

—In 2000, 55 percent of the population was African American, 24 percent Latino, 16 percent Other, 4 percent White, 1 percent Asian (DSNI, 2003)

—The per-capita income for the Dudley neighborhood in 1999 was $12,332, and 45 percent of Dudley families had yearly incomes below $25,000 (Bacon, Russell, and Tighe 2003, p. 24)

According to the U.S. Census Bureau, 29 percent of Dudley residents live in poverty, but the number of poor families is actually much higher.

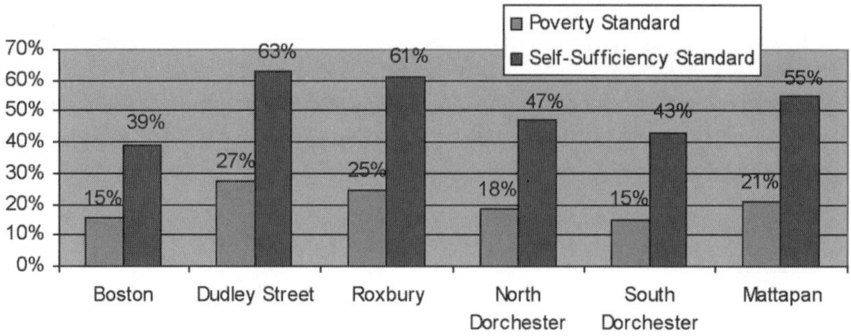

Family households in poverty vs. households living below self-sufficiency standard. (Data source: J. Bacon, L. H. Russell, and J. Tighe, 2003)

The federal poverty standard does not reflect the cost of housing, or regional differences in the cost of living per state. The poverty standard for a family of four, $18,244, cannot possibly support such a family, especially in Boston. According to the Family Economic Self-Sufficiency Standard (FESS)—a measure that "takes into account the costs of housing, food, transportation, child care, health care, miscellaneous expenses and taxes, and calculates the amount of money it takes for a family to meet basic needs without outside assistance from either the government or family and friends" (2003, p. 6)—a family of four in the Dudley neighborhood needs an income of $54,600 to be self-sufficient. Sixty-three percent of Dudley households fall below this self-sufficiency standard (Bacon, Russell, and Tighe, 2003). Clearly, this is a community that needs support.

History of Project Hope

Medoff's and Sklar's *Streets of Hope: The Fall and Rise of an Urban Neighborhood* (1994) notes the significant role of the Little Sisters of the Assumption (LSA) at Project Hope who have helped organize families and bring about positive changes in the Dudley area for half a century. From 1947 to 1960 the sisters who lived in the Project Hope convent on Magnolia Street provided home health care and social work services for Dudley residents in crisis. In an interview, Sister Margaret Leonard, Project Hope's executive director, told me:

> In those earlier days when we were operating as Little Sisters of the Assumption, poverty was extremely different because when you looked at the '40s and '50s in many ways, we lived in an economy which was labor intensive and capital was national and we had some control over it. So

> you had people who were coming from other countries and they moved into jobs in the manufacturing arena that paid good salaries and good benefits. So you could get a job and you could move out of poverty. And that was really very different. There was a possibility that you could move up the ladder and a lot of those families did. But the as time went on, we moved into a capital-intensive market, which is where we are now.

In the 1970s, the Little Sisters witnessed the effects of unemployment, inadequate housing, and deepening poverty on Dudley residents who were suffering in the face of economic transformation, gentrification, and the racial violence that resulted from Boston's school desegregation efforts. They decided to expand their services in response to these needs and, in particular, to the increasing number of homeless families needing help. Before she came to Project Hope, Sister Margaret was the LSA's "provincial" (chief executive officer) in New York's East Harlem neighborhood. When she arrived in Boston, she met with the sisters living in the Magnolia Street convent and asked them what they felt should be done to address the neighborhood's problems, especially around housing issues. The sisters participated in many community meetings and "listened to the cries of people in the neighborhood."

Mina, who was a student at Project Hope between 1990 and 1993, recounted how the sisters reached out to the neighbors:

> I lived in my house across the street twenty-six years, so way before the program started, Project Hope has always been a family support for me. You know what I mean? They always let me know what was going on because they were always in my house, Thanksgiving time, Christmastime, or just visiting the neighborhood, kinda reaching out to the neighborhood. . . . [The nuns] had me get a petition, going around the neighborhood and saying, "How would you like the idea of us being a shelter? Because we didn't feel like we were supporting your neighborhood as much as we wanted to."

According to Sister Margaret, they determined that "We should really open this house up and bring the people in. And, that's how Project Hope got identified, the use of the word HOPE: House Open, People Enter."

In 1983, Project Hope became one of the first family shelters in the state of Massachusetts, and Sister Margaret was hired as its first executive director. It was soon considered the "Cadillac" of family shelters in Massachusetts, and became a favorite of Governor Michael Dukakis, who would often hold his press conferences about homelessness there. Project Hope staff believed community organizing was the key to addressing the neighborhood's problems. Sister Margaret and other Project Hope staffers worked with residents and staff at community-based organizations such as La Alianza Hispana and WAITThouse (We're All in This Together) to create the Dudley Street Neighborhood Initiative (DSNI):

> In 1984, Dudley residents came together to resist the patterns of abandonment and gentrification that had already pushed low-income people out of the South End and the West End. Redlining, disinvestments, and arson fires combined to physically and spiritually devastate this community, a devastation symbolized by 1,300 vacant lots. We refused to accept these conditions. At DSNI's founding meeting, residents declared our intention to control community land and services for the benefit of the community. (DSNI, 1996, p. 3)[1]

Sister Margaret worked with DSNI and Dudley residents to create programs that not only provided important social services to low-income families, but also inspired collective social action and positive community development. For example, in 1992 Sister Margaret, Sue Beaton (a member of the Board of Directors), and DSNI spearheaded a campaign to build the Magnolia Cooperative Housing, eight units of affordable housing across the street from Project Hope. In 1994, the Dorchester Bay Economic Development Corporation developed thirty-eight additional low-income units; each of the homes was built within a two-block radius of Project Hope. The majority of the new homeowners were women with children. The text on page 37 shows the evolution of Project Hope's programs.

At the time this research was conducted, all of Project Hope's programs—with the exception of the Transition to Work Collaborative—were based in the former Little Sisters of the Assumption convent at 45 Magnolia Street. This four-story building is an attractive, clean, welcoming space decorated with Afrocentric artwork. Upon entering, one finds the main office to the right, the shelter manager's office immediately on the left, and a reception area in the front hallway that also serves as the food pantry distribution area. The reception area is a few steps in from the front door and has several bulletin boards. On the left wall, a dry-erase board displays announcements about upcoming community meetings. Another bulletin board on the right wall has information about housing rights, apartment openings, and welfare advocacy. A third bulletin board advertises employment opportunities. Children's photographs and drawings hang on walls in the reception area.

The first floor also contains two classrooms for the Adult Learners Program, as well as a living room, dining room, and large kitchen for the families who live in Project Hope. The Children's Center is located in the back, in an annex. The basement houses three offices and four cubicles for teachers, volunteers, and community organizers who work with DSNI and other community groups, along with storage space, laundry

Project Hope's programs since the late 1960s

1970s	Red Cross courses
	English as a Second Language courses
	Community Meetings
	Youth groups and Patriot Girl Scouts
	Thrift shop for clothing
	Parenting groups
	Community gardens
	Food co-ops and food pantry
	In 1979, Family Shelter program began
1980s	Polling site for three years and voter registration activities
	In 1983, Project Hope officially opens as Boston's first family shelter
	Child care center
	Housing search
	In 1984, Dudley Street Neighborhood Initiative founded
	Collaboration with Uphams Corner Health Center
1990s	Adult Learning Center
	Magnolia Cooperative Housing Development
	Project FLAIR/Transition to Work Collaborative
	Family Child Care micro-enterprise
	National accreditation for Children's Center
	Homeless Prevention program
	Homes for Families founded
2000s	One Family Scholars Program
	In 2006, Project Hope moves to new building on Dudley Street

facilities, and a large classroom. The second floor has additional staff offices, including the offices of the executive director, development director, family services coordinators, and finance department. The homeless families live on the third floor in eight small bedrooms equipped with sinks. Each room is furnished differently, depending on the size of the family, but the majority have twin-sized bunk beds. The families share a large bathroom containing three showers. Outside the bedrooms is a communal space with toys, a couch, and a small television.

The family shelter has twenty-two beds for homeless families, and they are always occupied and in demand. On a typical morning, upon entering the building, one can smell bacon frying in the kitchen and hear the laughter, and crying, of children who enter the front of the building on their way to the Children's Center. Busy, tired-looking mothers who live in the shelter feed their children breakfast while others check their mailboxes or meet in the hallway with a house manager to discuss the day's activities. Overall, Project Hope looks and feels like a home. Unlike many family shelters, there are no restrictions on length of stay. On average there are eight families living in the shelter, and their length of stay ranges from three months to a year, depending upon the availability of affordable housing and the successful acquisition of state or federal housing subsidies. There are "shelter rules" about cleanliness (the women must do chores), visitors (visiting hours are between 1:00 P.M. and 8:00 P.M.), housing search activities (the women must work with the housing advocate to search for affordable, permanent housing), and mandatory weekly "house meetings" at which a meal is shared by all.

The Adult Learners Program has three classrooms. The main classroom is located in the former chapel, across from the living room on the first floor. It has three large bay windows with a southern exposure that admits an abundance of sunlight. It seats twenty-five, and the furniture consists of large round tables, comfortable chairs, carpeting, attractive artwork and posters, plants, and several bookcases filled with novels and books related to social justice issues. The main classroom also has a tiny kitchen with a refrigerator, stove, and microwave for the adult learners and faculty. A sliding door separates the main classroom from a second smaller classroom that serves as a computer lab and tutoring space. A third windowless classroom is located in the basement. It has round tables in the center, two bookcases, and two long tables that hold boxes of neighborhood organizing materials. In the evenings this classroom is used by community groups, so it also stores signs and posters about Patriot Girl Scouts, Project SHARE (a food co-op), DSNI, and other projects and community events.

The Development of the Adult Learners Program

> Would you like to:
> * Get your high school diploma?
> * Improve your English, reading, writing, math?
>
> It is never too late to learn!
> Classes are small. Program is 20 hours a week, Mon.–Fri. 9 A.M.–1 P.M.
> Childcare and transportation provided free.
> Classes begin Tuesday Sept. 3rd
> Make an appointment to come and find out more about this program.
> Student quotes:
> "My goal for the future is to receive my certificate and get a good job. I am glad I'm enrolled in this program because it is helping me to reach this goal."
> "Each class is a positive experience for me"
> "Thanks Project Hope for making it easier for me and my child." (From the Adult Learners Program's first advertisement)

In the summer of 1990, Sister Beatrice Patrick, working with a follow-up group that met biweekly at Project Hope, asked former shelter residents what they needed, now that they had housing. The six women unanimously agreed that they wanted a GED program at Project Hope. Because there were already a few GED programs in the neighborhood, Sister Margaret was initially opposed to developing another. However, the formerly homeless women convinced her and the Board of Directors. Sister Margaret explained that until the late 1980s the majority of Project Hope's programs were focused on the families who lived in the shelter, but there was a growing movement within Project Hope to serve the wider community. They wanted to open their doors to families "on the verge of losing their housing." She explained, "We always had a food, clothing, and referral program for families in the neighborhood, but with the creation of the adult learner center we opened it to neighborhood families and those in the shelter. . . . We decided to look at Project Hope as a community resource center." As programs expanded within the house, the sisters needed more space and were fortunate to acquire property one block up on Magnolia Street. When the nuns moved out of the convent, their old bedrooms on the second floor were converted to offices.

Having listened and responded to the community's request for adult education classes, Project Hope opened the ALP in October 1990. With six students and three volunteer teachers, it was a humble beginning. Sister Joan Ward, a Sister of Notre Dame, focused her energies on securing funding from the Massachusetts Department of Education in order to sustain the program's future. She also hired Sister Lois as the program's first director. Sister Lois spent her early days doing "homework" by visiting and observing various local adult education programs such as Bridge Over Troubled Waters, WAITThouse, and Odwin Learning Center. When Sister Lois first started working at Project Hope, she was a seasoned elementary schoolteacher, but she had no adult education experience. She told me she did not "even know what the letters GED stood for." She used a curriculum from the Dorchester Youth Collaborative for ex-offenders and adapted lessons and Individualized Educational Plans (IEPs) for the Project Hope women.

Sister Lois told me that at first she did not feel comfortable discussing the women's personal problems in classes, and she did not expect the women to repeatedly raise issues related to violence, drug addiction, and other problems. She believes that because the first cohort of students was accustomed to participating in Sister Beatrice's follow-up support group, they were empowered to express their concerns and advocate for their education and other needs. Mahogany was a student in 1991 and described the program as a "psychiatric session." She told me:

> Project Hope I found was more of a psychiatric session as well as a educational session, and I think that's what made *my* time at Project Hope, the era that we were in, better than any other era. I think, later on they got more educational and forgot about the personal time. I think in anything you need to have personal, and you need education, too. You know? And I think that was the best part about Sister Lois and Robin and all them. Because, not only were they educated, but they wasn't afraid to be personal, either. Which made a lot of the women more open to saying, okay, you know [somber and reflective] "I really can't read." Because somebody in the group would say, "I don't understand that." Oh, "You don't understand that either?" Okay, "Well I don't understand it either."

Though Mahogany emphasized the "personal," her narrative makes it clear that the "personal" was in fact a key factor in fostering a positive experience with "education."

In her first conversation with the women learners, Sister Lois remembers saying, "So this is the group that really wants to get this program off the ground? What do you think it needs?" She told them she would share "some of the things I have learned," and asked them "'What do you think about this?' They were wide-open and enthusiastic and said, 'Let's go!'" Sister Lois told them she was an inexperienced GED teacher: "This is brand new to me. I feel okay about that if you do. And, we'll have to create this together . . . and whatever happens will have to happen, and we'll have to keep learning and growing and changing." She recalled how the women and Sister Joan tried to make the classroom a very welcoming environment: "The sisters were willing to convert a chapel. Really, you have to realize how much importance that might have had to some older sisters, you know?"

Sister Lois described herself as a traditional, "structured" teacher who was not "loose." She taught most of the classes in the beginning and then recruited Robin Jones, a mathematics professor at a local community college, and Nina Robinson, a professional musician, who volunteered to teach writing, literature, and science. Carolyn Greene and Teresa Thompson from the Women's Theological Center joined soon thereafter. Other volunteer teachers during the program's early years were feminists, Catholic sisters, and mission volunteers who developed woman-centered approaches in their classes and experimented with projects and classroom activities that incorporated the social problems the women faced. With limited resources and a diversity of literacy skills among the women,

Sister Lois encouraged peer teaching, so students worked together in pairs or small groups to complete multilevel classroom activities. This collaborative learning process inspired a spirit of community, where everyone was learning together and helping one another. The students fully appreciated this pedagogy, as Mina's account shows:

> They always would work one-on-one. That was the main thing, working one-on-one, and you could always ask questions. And we did group things, we worked together with each other, or else the teacher would come around and work with each one of us, individually. And we could always ask questions. And they'd never rush through anything, they always wait until you were ready for the next step. Know what I mean? You never felt pressured, that was the main thing for me is not to feel overwhelmed and that I couldn't do it.

A Collective Growth Process

In July 1991, Project Hope created and became the lead agency in the Project FLAIR (Family Literacy an Adult Integrated Response) network. Project FLAIR was a collaboration of family shelters within a five-mile radius of Project Hope, with the goal of "educating shelter residents through outreach, educational assessment and referral, as well as follow-up and basic family literacy opportunities." The Project FLAIR family shelters, led by Project Hope, focused on assessing the educational needs of the homeless adults living in their shelters. For a brief period, transportation to and from Project Hope was provided for shelter residents who needed a high school equivalency, or basic literacy skills. According to data from Project FLAIR, 90 percent of the women students were between the ages of eighteen and thirty, and, on average, they had two children aged six and under. Eighty-five percent of the shelter residents were African American, 8 to 10 percent were Hispanic, and fewer than 1 percent were Haitian, African, or white. Eighty-seven percent of the homeless adult learners involved in Project FLAIR had left school before their sixteenth birthday, 50 percent read at or below the fourth-grade level, and 4 percent were functionally illiterate. In the first year, more than two hundred adults were introduced to Project FLAIR. Participants were expected to develop five-year plans and participate in mentoring groups. In 1993, 60 percent of FLAIR adults were enrolled in some sort of community program, including GED at Project Hope. Project Hope and the other collaborating shelters were able to reach more than two hundred homeless adults through Project FLAIR.

The Project FLAIR network received its first funding in January 1992 through the Massachusetts Department of Education McKinney Project, which was supported by the 1987 Stewart B. McKinney Homeless Assistance Act (Public Law 100-77) (Bachtel, 1999). The McKinney Act allotted funds to states to offer educational programs for homeless adults.[2] According to Norris and Kennington (1992), "a state-by-state review of the Stewart B. McKinney funded educational initiatives, revealed 28 educational techniques or approaches other than traditional basic skills remediation or GED preparation" (p. 21). The materials developed in these "nontraditional" programs were primarily "learner-centered" in that the learners themselves expressed needs for particular subject areas (p. 21; also see Sperazi, 1990). The ALP program design and curriculum, modeled by Sister Lois on the Dorchester Youth Collaborative, clearly fell into this category of "nontraditional" and "learner-centered":

> A clear preference is given to individualized instruction to: customize instruction to match student's skill strengths and weaknesses; to be attentive to particular learning styles; to better monitor each student's progress; to provide an alternative model of learning to many students who have experienced (and failed) in traditional all-the-time whole-class instruction; to avoid boredom or frustration caused when students have to listen to what they already know or are expected to grasp material for which they lack readiness. Large group instruction is also used because: members of a group can learn a great deal from one another's perceptions, ideas, insights, judgments, etc. regardless of reading or math levels; exclusive use of one to one instruction can be isolating; group experiences help students realize they are part of a community and help them to understand interpersonal relationships. (ALP Archives)

But Adult Education Homeless (AEH) programs, such as the ALP, faced significant challenges. Norris and Kennington (1992) describe how the administration of McKinney funds by state education agencies led to "Tension [between] accountability requirements and the realities of providing educational opportunities to homeless adults" (p. 10). Specific issues for Project Hope included Massachusetts Department of Education guidelines about class set-up procedures, attendance requirements, and standardized assessment policies that could not accurately reflect real barriers to participation and learning, such as trauma and learning disabilities (Norris and Kennington, 1992, pp. 11–12). The majority of the women who participated in the ALP had experienced some form of family violence, and health issues such as depression and posttraumatic stress posed obstacles to their learning and attainment of life goals (see chapter 3).

In terms of accountability measures such as attendance and completion of the GED, the ALP was not a "success" in the eyes of the Massachusetts Department of Education. Between 1995 and 1998, only eighteen of the fifty women I interviewed obtained their GEDs. This low rate of GED attainment is not surprising, given that 82 percent of the women had attended and dropped out of at least one other Adult Basic Education (ABE) program before they enrolled in the ALP. (Retention rates in ABE are very low in general.) The primary reason Project Hope women had left other ABE programs was their inability to meet strict attendance policies. The homeless mothers had to manage school, work, and family responsibilities, as well as comply with the demands of the Department of Transitional Assistance (DTA) and the rules of the shelters where they lived. The women often had scheduling conflicts that made it difficult for them to attend school regularly. For example, some welfare caseworkers would schedule meetings for their clients, and then penalize them if they missed these appointments. In addition, other shelters referred homeless women to the Adult Learners Program, often mandating that they participate in educational activities or risk losing public assistance. A few of the women with whom I spoke felt they were judged negatively by other homeless women who thought that "I don't want to learn," or that they were attending school "to keep welfare out of my case."

By 1993, the ALP had been in operation for three years and teachers had learned some important lessons. Feminist teachers and missionary volunteers (Little Sisters of the Assumption, Sisters of Notre Dame, and Notre Dame AmeriCorps) had been recruited, and these teachers desired a deeper focus on women-centered learning and political empowerment through critical literacy. In a "Proposal to take the next step in the development of the Adult Learning Program at Project Hope," submitted to the Project Hope Board of Directors in November 1993, Sister Lois and Robin Jones wrote:

> Over the past 3 years the ALP has met the educational needs of women who are or were homeless with a program aimed at enabling the woman to get her GED. As we worked together with the women who came to Project Hope and listened to their needs, we saw that the GED program, as taught in most other sites in this area, was not helpful to many of these women. Successful completion required that the woman develop and apply skills to aspects of literature, social studies, and science in which she had little sense of context. Women also come to the program with a variety of life experiences and skills, many of which are not recognized in a traditional GED program. In such a setting, women become

> frustrated with the learning process because they do not feel valued for who they are and what they have struggled to become.

The teachers wanted to help women gain literacy skills in a meaningful context. They requested funds to "research models for integrated curricula with adult learners and share that information with learners and teachers in the Adult Learning program with the goal of having such a curriculum in place September 1994." Teachers identified the following successful instructional elements:

> —We use learner-centered approaches to provide our adult learners with an opportunity to have control over at least one aspect of their lives.
> —We use adult learners' life experiences as the basis for curriculum and learning activities.
> —We develop curricula that address the diversity of the group such as age, race, ethnicity, sexuality, and others.
> —We use varied educational materials that recognize a variety of learning styles and multiple intelligences.
> —We engage in on-going assessment to measure and identify student progress towards their learning goals. As a group, teachers meet regularly to facilitate the sharing of curricula, instructional materials, and reflection on our practices.
> —Individually and as a group teachers engage in on-going staff development focusing on areas such as literacy instruction, welfare and homelessness issues, accessing community resources for adult learners, and integrating health issues into the curriculum. (ALP Archives)

To achieve these curricular goals, the proposal also requested financial support to hire a consultant (Robin Jones) who would research and secure additional funding.

In 1994 Project Hope received a five-year grant from the Massachusetts Department of Education. With a 50 percent increase in funding, the program began to grow in size and in the scope of educational activities it offered. With more resources in professional development, Project Hope hired more teachers, who developed critical literacy and popular education classes. With welfare reform impending, the program had a growing waiting list because women on welfare were rushing to finish their GEDs before their benefits were terminated. During this time period (mid-1990s), which also saw an increasingly politicized discourse on welfare reform, Project Hope's staff also began to organize in the community to resist punitive welfare reform.

The Spirit of Advocacy, Collaboration, and Resistance

Although Project Hope had worked with many community-based organizations throughout the city and state, the era of welfare reform strengthened networks of support and collaboration among social service providers in the Dudley community and across the state's poorest communities. The Project Hope women played an important role in organized resistance to the proposed welfare laws. According to Sister Margaret, "Advocacy is a part of everything we do. . . . With the implementation of the welfare reform stuff here in the state, women were getting calls all over the place about you have to give up adult education, you have to go back to work. You have to go to work or you have to go into a community service job. And that's what people were hearing all over the place and they were dropping out of these educational programs and all." Sister Margaret and Project Hope's staff felt that the Dudley Street Neighborhood Initiative area and the neighborhood were "a political entity that could really get some political movement." She asked staff to "call a meeting with all the different agencies here and see how we should respond to it. So we did. Then, as people realized that we were doing this, people came from a number of other places as well to these meetings. And we kind of developed together what we felt was an alternative education and training program for women." On March 28, 1996, a group of concerned social service providers, academics, low-income women, and activists met at the Alexander Street Co-op to "Build an alternative education, training, jobs program." The group brainstormed the "essential" elements of such a program. Their vision was broad-reaching and thorough.

There was outraged response to the DTA's community service requirement and organized resistance to workfare requirements. The strategic continuum document produced by the "Alternatives" group asked people to: "Challenge current workfare regulations and develop consensus on the true meaning of 'community service'—e.g. caring for a disabled parent is not accepted under current workfare regulations, although many recipients and agencies view this as a valuable service to the community." They also proposed to "build coordinated refusal on part of all employers to participate in workfare." The organizers argued that the foundations of an effective resistance movement included: "Building a broad based coalition with other city/state groups working to resist the reform" and "Building critical understanding of the welfare system and the political forces controlling it."

Common elements of an alternative education, training, and jobs program

Assessments	—In-depth and participative. —Comprehensive: attitudes, skills, reading levels, basic education, pre-GED, GED, higher education, connecting with real jobs with fair livable wages and benefits that are family/child friendly. —Educative and voluntary: individualized plans for different skills, needs, and abilities.
Child Care	—High quality, affordable, and available. —Flexible, on-site, full-time during training, education, and work. —Long-term and reliable. —Transportation provided. —Child-friendly employers. —After-school programs (that help school-age children with homework/study skills).
Health Care	—Family health insurance benefits. —Health insurance (guaranteed and affordable).
Education	—Providing a range of options: Adult Basic Education (accounting and budgeting to access to higher education and higher wages). —Tuition assistance and long-term possibilities. —Four-year college.
Training	—Training programs with building blocks to next steps. —Quality training/educational programs that teach useful and marketable skills. —Training that leads to fair livable wages and benefits. —Training that is inclusive of real-life experience on job placements.
Jobs	—Job placement services: based upon real assessments, provide access to options, job fairs, meeting people in workplace/connected job placements, support services, follow-through, and customer driven. —Jobs that lead to fair, livable wages and benefits (paid vacations, union jobs). —Potential for growth in the job. —Create real life (on-the-job experience and training). —Connected to higher education.

Essential Criteria for Education, Training, and Jobs (Building Blocks/Components)

—Voluntary choice and tailored to the individual.
—Addresses needs of the whole family (inclusive of fathers).
—Family and child friendly.
—Mentoring and support services/teams, especially for single mothers (substance abuse prevention, education, and support services).
—Flexibility: ability to move in and out of a program.
—Programs adaptable to diverse learning styles.
—Looser time frames, with willingness to be accountable.
—Long-term funding for program.
—Respectful and rooted in communities, with community support and control.
—Involvement of all: advocates, providers, and recipients.
—Include low-income workers.
—Better training for welfare and other workers and give correct information.

Shared concerns about the impact of welfare reform and already stretched resources led to the development of the Transition to Work Collaborative (TTWC). The TTWC held its first planning meeting on October 15, 1996, with the goal of expanding and improving a "continuum of care" among the various programs that provided education, training, and social services to homeless families. Again, Project Hope was the lead agency, and the TTWC agencies included many of the same partners as Project FLAIR. This collaboration of eight shelter and service providers (it eventually grew to ten) proposed to provide a "Continuum of care in the area of education and economic development services." According to a May 7, 1996, proposal to the City of Boston, TTWC outlined the need to fill "gaps" by "Assisting families to assess themselves and develop an economic development plan; providing education and information about the economy and available education and training resources; providing access to needed education and training; and providing support and advocacy to ensure that family, health, and legal issues all support families' economic development goals" (ALP Archives). The TTWC used a "participatory assessment model" to set goals with shelter residents and addressed the essential elements of an alternative education and training program described above. For example, the TTWC model included six-week economic literacy classes for shelter residents in which the women learned how to develop and maintain a budget, as well as about their rights, changes in welfare legislation, credit, and banking. They also received counseling and referrals to educational and job opportunities. The women worked with a "career advocate" (who was usually a formerly homeless woman) to implement their economic development plans after the economic literacy classes ended. They met in monthly peer group meetings and individually with their career advocate.

From 1995 to 1997, Project Hope produced a video documentary titled *Women of Strength: Four Stories from the Welfare Debate.* The idea for the video came from a group of Project Hope women who were outraged about unfair and negative stereotyping of welfare recipients in the media. In 1995, an advisory committee was formed and Leah Mahan (producer of *Holding Ground,* a documentary about DSNI) agreed to produce a video that would address the misconceptions shaping the welfare debate by presenting facts, confronting stereotypes, and "humanizing" the debate with stories of real people. The four formerly homeless women featured in the documentary were all past residents of Project Hope and were eager to share their experiences. After the *Women of Strength* video was completed in 1997, I worked with the women in the Adult Learners Program to develop a viewer's guide for the *Women of Strength* video.

The viewer's guide inspired the development of the Women's Economic Justice Project (WEJP). The goals of the WEJP were to: 1) train and pay welfare recipients as lay welfare rights advocates and community legal education trainers (a model curriculum was developed specifically for this purpose by Greater Boston Legal Services and Northeastern University's Poverty Law Clinic); 2) build active grassroots participation in legislative reform by strengthening community collaborations with city and statewide policy advocacy groups; 3) reach out to communities beyond our own, using *Women of Strength* to challenge perceptions of the causes of poverty. Roberta Cavalos, Project Hope's social worker, described the direct relationship between Project Hope's literacy and advocacy efforts:

> The structures and causes of economic injustice must be challenged by education, strong community leaders, and united grassroots activism. The WEJP is an innovative model of how a community-based direct service provider uses its resources, power, and outreach capacity to act as a catalyst and a key forum for organizing, leadership development, and political education in the neighborhood. The vision of the WEJP is simple. A mother who can't read or who needs shelter won't attend a meeting on welfare rights. She will look for shelter and for a literacy class—so we organize through direct services. We meet the family's immediate need—build a relationship on a one by one basis, and then we organize. Our goal goes far beyond the alleviation of immediate needs.

Project Hope Today

Project Hope's conjoined commitments to social needs and social justice, and especially to poor and homeless women and families, can be seen in the following list of their current services. Besides the ALP, Project Hope offers:

—On-site child care in a nationally accredited, state-licensed Children's Center. All shelter residents automatically receive free "slots" for child care in the Children's Center. The Children's Center also has a Family Literacy program that involves parents in their children's education, as well as specialists who work with children who have experienced violence;

—On-site Food Pantry and Clothing Donations. The food pantry is also open to the community, and some women learn about the ALP via their contact with the Food Pantry;

—On-site housing search assistance and advocacy with the housing search advocate, who provides information about housing subsidies and tenants' rights;

—On-site health care with a visiting nurse from Boston's Health Care for the Homeless. These services are targeted to shelter residents primarily. However, some health services, such as flu shots, blood pressure screening, and mammograms, are available to all;

—On-site access to career counseling, welfare advocacy, and job search services through the Transition to Work Collaborative, along with access to higher education via the Women in Community Development program (collaboration with the Women's Institute for Housing and Economic Development and the University of Massachusetts-Boston), a college program for formerly homeless women and low-income women who are interested in human services careers. The university waives tuition for the women in exchange for faculty provided by Project Hope;

—Access to substance abuse treatment and services, health services, and mental health services through the Comprehensive Health Education project, which has links to each of the neighborhood health centers. Weekly health workshops based on women's questions are offered in the ALP; and

—Access to legal counseling and immigration advocacy through the on-site Neighborhood Development program. The Neighborhood Development program also provides education about welfare reform, voter awareness and registration, neighborhood crime watch, community gardening, and other issues identified by Project Hope's community organizers, who are former adult learners.

It should be clear from this history and description that Project Hope facilitates positive changes in the lives of homeless women and their children, and in the broader Dudley community. Sister Margaret believes that the religious foundation of their work has been crucial to Project Hope's success:

> I think what really helped us in terms of our history here at Project Hope was the fact that there were two religious women's congregations that were instrumental of what became Project Hope. And both the Sisters of Notre Dame and ourselves are international congregations who have a global perspective in terms of poverty. And, because we are religious women who have gone through a process of saying that we've been influenced by the feminist agenda. We were influenced by the liberation agenda. And, we went through a process in which we looked at the structures of our own society that were patriarchal and hierarchical and we changed them.

Sister Lois agrees that the synergy between the Little Sisters of the Assumption and the Sisters of Notre Dame has generated "a very interesting relationship":

> In one way you have a whole group of people who are identified as educators and whose mission is really to the poor and most neglected places [the Sisters of Notre Dame]. . . . Then you have a group of women who

> are really social workers and nurses primarily here [Little Sisters of the Assumption]. Both of us are working with the community, the neighborhood women, and with that comes a holistic model for working and understanding people. . . . We feel called to be in this place. We need to be in this place. This is where we want to invest our lives, you know. We need to listen to the people among whom we're walking. It's not a talk-down kind of focus. We need to be in a posture of being really good listeners.

The "philosophy of homelessness" written by Sister Joan illustrates the critical perspective the nuns share regarding the structural causes of poverty: "Homelessness is a by-product of the economy and of negative housing policies of the federal government. The combination of these factors has resulted in a dearth of affordable housing. The absence of alternative affordable housing options has resulted in homelessness. As the situation continues, homelessness is increasingly accompanied by hopelessness." Inspiring hope among low-income families is one of the things Project Hope does best. Through its collaborations with other community-based organizations, its sensitive ears to the expressed needs of low-income women in the community, and its mission to address structural causes of poverty, Project Hope provides the ideal context for transformative learning, women's empowerment, and positive social change. In Sister Margaret's words:

> We try to empower these women, because we recognize that the women who are with us should be participants in shaping their own destinies and not have things imposed on them outside. Any programs we create, therefore, have their active involvement. It's important that victims of poverty and oppression and homelessness not internalize their situation in such a way as to blame themselves. Instead, the thrust is for them to understand the causes and forces behind the situation and to act with us as advocates for change at the level of cause.

In the next chapter, "Mothering in the War Years," I turn to the Project Hope women themselves. The women describe the poverty-related problems that affect their everyday lives and pose barriers to their education, including homelessness, health problems, drug addiction, sexual abuse, and family violence. According to Rockhill (1993), "it is not so much a question of whether literacy 'in fact' makes any difference in women's [in]dependence as it is the symbolic vision of education as transforming one's life, transporting one into the 'safety' of the middle-class home, white picket fence and all. And education may be 'in reality' women's only ticket out of poverty—and it may not make a difference" (p. 349). She questions whether education can end cycles of violence in women's lives, asking, is literacy enough? The next chapters explore the difference that literacy makes in the lives of poor women.

3 *Mothering in the War Years*

> People drop out of school for a reason. It's not because they want to drop out. I mean, [if the] GED's there, they have to take advantage of it. And some people give up, when they close the doors. They give up and they stay on the system. Would they prefer for them people to stay on the system, or for the people to go to GED, and get their life together, get a job, or whatever the case is? . . . I'm still struggling with the GED. But, I'm gonna move up. I don't really want to stay where I'm at. I don't see myself there five years. I want to have more than that, so I still need that GED there.
>
> —Jessica

When Jessica made these comments in the spring of 2005, I had not seen her in seven years. Jessica dropped out of Project Hope's Adult Learners Program in 1998, after failing the GED math test repeatedly. Although she only needed three more points to pass the GED, her severe math anxiety posed a serious obstacle. She had four young children, her welfare benefits were about to be terminated, and the father of her kids was physically abusive. Jessica succumbed to the pressure of diminished support: she faced limits on both the number of times she could take the GED within a year and on how many months she could continue receiving welfare benefits for her family. So, she quit school again in order to work a full-time job as a medical records clerk at a local hospital. Jessica told me she continues to work on her GED math with a tutor on weekends. She had taken the GED math test in November 2004, but she would now have to take all five tests again because her scores had expired. Still, Jessica is persistent and has not given up hope that someday she will finish her GED and "move up" in the world.

Jessica's story exemplifies both the struggles and the determination that characterized the women in the ALP. As a welfare mother in an abusive relationship, Jessica faced enormous obstacles in her efforts to get an education and make a better life for her family. Yet she persisted in those efforts, unwavering in her focus on moving forward. This chapter profiles the women in the ALP in their own voices, taken from interviews and education histories. The women tell of lifelong poverty-related problems that continue to affect their everyday lives: childhood trauma and abuse, difficulties in school, teen pregnancy, domestic violence, and isolation in adulthood. Indeed, a significant finding of this study pertains to the prevalence and persistence of violence in the lives of homeless mothers, beginning in childhood and continuing to the present: 64 percent of the women reported past experiences with violence; 69 percent of the violence reported was domestic violence. In addition, all the women in the ALP were or had been homeless. The barriers described here are consistent with those documented by other researchers who have studied poor women's lives (Stack, 1974; Liebow, 1993; Polakow, 1993; Passaro, 1996; Edin and Lein, 1997; Way, 1998; Brandwein, 1999; Dodson, 1999).

Just like Jessica, however, the women were determined to move forward. No matter how others viewed them, they held onto their beliefs in themselves. Delila said,

> I never pictured myself to be in a shelter. You know, I used to work. I had money and I never had a problem. I mean, I'm the kind of person who struggled to make a better living even as a little girl. . . . Everybody was against me. You know, I didn't have friends. I didn't have nobody to support me. Not the welfare office or my worker. Everybody was like, you know how you treat, you throw your garbage around? I was like that. But I said to myself, "I'm not gonna sit down and feel sorry for myself. I'm gonna find an apartment any way I can." And it was very hard.

Like Delila, each of the women I met at Project Hope had worked, or were working, and were striving to improve their economic situations. Many explicitly named their children as their motivation. As participants in the ALP, the women had high hopes for the futures of their families. Yet, as I will show, they faced significant personal and societal barriers to their education and social mobility.

Early Childhood Trauma

Sixty percent of the women in this study reported early childhood trauma. Both education histories and interviews revealed numerous instances in which parents were killed, or died from drug abuse or domestic violence. Ten women lost their mother or father when they were children (under the age of eighteen), and of these deaths, four were homicides. In addition, four women reported having been abandoned by their mothers, four reported having run away from their home or foster homes when they were teenagers, and several others reported other childhood traumas, including illnesses and abusive parents who were alcoholics or drug addicts.

The death of a mother or father clearly had a profound impact on the women, as evidenced by the pain and emotional reactions during interviews and reflections in their writings:

> *Coletta:* My mother and I never got along. She beat me because I looked like my father. She was not there for me. My stepfather was the only one that understood me. I was so hurt when he was killed. I couldn't believe it. I felt that he was the only one I could talk to.
>
> *Soledad:* My father passed away when I was a child. When I grew up I started asking questions about my father, and my mother told me that he had killed himself when I was very small. I asked her, "Why did he kill himself?" But she did not give me any information about what really happened.

Yvette was deeply hurt when she learned how her mother actually died, after her aunt gave her a tape recording from her mother:

> At first they were saying that my mom died of pneumonia. But then, I guess that was my family telling me because they didn't really want me to be hurt. But, back in '87 we really didn't know what AIDS was. . . . [crying] It hurts me because I could just imagine what my mother was going through, the pain that she was feeling. Knowing that she was gonna die and that we was there. And she always used to tell us that she loved us. Every day we used to go over there and she used to tell us that she loved us, you know? And I kinda knew that she was gonna die but I didn't think that it was gonna happen all so soon.

That death was often accompanied by secrecy and withholding compounded the trauma for these women.

Sexual abuse was another consistent thread in the women's histories, and it too was generally (and not surprisingly) kept secret:

> *Mahogany:* At the age of nine, I got my period. I was not ready for that mentally or physically and I was expected to be a girl who knew how to act with this new thing. When I returned home one day my mother sent me to the mailbox to get some mail. . . . So I proceeded to take the elevator to the basement floor where the man was standing, an older man, about mid 40s–50s. It looked like it always did, people coming

> in from the cold to get warm, etc. So when he raped me, it was a blow to the mind and still is. I never told my mother. It may seem stupid but it was the right thing for me to do at age nine.

These traumatic experiences and their consequences made establishing trust a significant challenge for a number of the women, which in turn affected their participation in the ALP. I found that the women's experiences with rape, incest, and child abuse had long-term effects on their ability to trust others, to feel safe in the classroom, and to participate in class discussions. This research is consistent with Horsman's (2000) work on the impact of violence and early childhood trauma on Canadian women who participated in adult basic education classes.

Dropping Out

Despite their painful childhoods, many of the women were happy in school when they were young. But by high school, the complexities of their lives and their school experiences led them to drop out. Again, the research accurately contextualizes their experiences. In this chapter's opening quote, Jessica suggests that people drop out "for a reason." According to Beder (1991), "The available evidence suggests that for most school leavers, dropping out represents a rational and often unavoidable response to difficult situations rather than personal failure" (p. 71). Beder found that the most common reason for adult learners to drop out was that they had to work and needed to earn income. Quigley (1989) writes that "illiterates leave school not because they are failures, but because their cultures of orientation conflict with school culture in ways that become intolerable" (quoted in Beder, 1991, p. 72). Other studies suggest that there are multiple factors that can be linked to a student dropping out, including recent migration, being retained in a grade, and family poverty (Dodson, 1999; Fine, 1991; Fine and Zane, 1991). Fine (1991) finds that "attributes" of schools—such as teacher-student ratios, teacher turnover rates, disciplinary procedures, and high truancy rates—often affect dropout rates more than characteristics of individual students (p. 22). Fine adds that "the category of 'family problems' is one repeated often by educators and policymakers as a primary reason that low-income youngsters drop out" (p. 77).

Other research explains that high school dropouts, especially racial and ethnic minorities, often resist participating in adult education because they have had negative experiences in school (Cervero and Fitzpatrick, 1990; Quigley, 1992; Sparks, 1998). However, research by Reder and Strawn (2001) challenges the conception of "school resister" and the notion that the majority of high school dropouts have had negative schooling experiences. They argue that efforts to increase recruitment and retention of adult learners should not "assume that negative experiences are a common barrier" (p. 4).

In fact, many of the Project Hope women had fond memories of elementary school. However, when they went to high school, they began to have problems, or existing problems worsened. This is consistent with much research on urban high school dropouts (Fine, 1991; Way, 1998). For example, in a focus group, a number of the women described themselves as good students:

> *Lucky:* As for me, I learned a lot in elementary school. I was always "A" student, always won little merit awards. Always the little ones, you know. I learned a lot from elementary school.
>
> *Tashawna:* Me too. Elementary school, I had a good time. I was a good student all the way from kindergarten to the eighth grade.
>
> *Lucky:* I was always teacher's pet.
>
> *Tashawna:* Me too. All my teachers liked me. Yeah, I was like one of the pets.

Yvette described how she received awards in elementary school and was loved by her teachers, but had a hard time making the transition to high school:

> Math and reading was my favorite subject and I had certificates and awards and all that from math. . . . I'm talking about from third grade, all the teachers loved me. I mean, I could remember all their names now. And they used to love me and as I was growing up they would just tell me, "You're gonna be good at this, you're gonna be good at that." And when I got to middle school, I say yeah, they wasn't lying. You know, the elementary teachers were telling me the truth. I'm good at this and I'm good at that. And then when I got to high school, that's when all the problems start getting because at middle school it was the greatest, you don't have too much attention on you because you're in between, you know? But when you get to high school, you're like you wanna feel like the third grade is, when you're really in the eighth and the ninth grade. So it's, it's a lot of tension. And the fact that there was a lot of tension in there and then I was having problems with my mom and all that, it was not easy for me when I got to high school.

Similarly, Lucky explains how, when she went to high school, her good grades "went kapoof" as she got distracted by teenage life:

> In elementary school, I always won merit awards, the little medals with the flag in the middle right here [points to her left shoulder]. I have like ten of them. I was A and B student in middle and elementary school. High

> school, that's when I started getting the Bs and the Cs and Ds and then it went kapoof. . . . I used to be in this little Spanish crew. Called the P.C. Crew, Puerto Rican crew. There was about fifteen of us girls and we was always against another set of girls. Yeah, we was in this program . . . it was on the third floor that had a red side and a blue side. We was on the red side. The red side was called Home Base. Home Base, those are for people, like for myself, who didn't want to put their mind to the books, who just wanted to mess around, who was always getting in trouble. And it was like, one little room that they would keep us in eight hours a day to make sure we wouldn't get into trouble. But we would still get into trouble! We would go on the other side where we wasn't supposed to be to mess with the other girls. So it's like, it depends who you hang out, who you be with in school. Like I hang around with the wrong crowd in school. You know, they got me into trouble. They got me into drinking, they got me into smoking weed. They got me into stealing cars. There was this one friend of mine, Jill, me and her dropped out at the same time. It was like we followed each other. We hooked school together. We got a boyfriend at the same time together. We dropped out of school together. We got pregnant together. We done everything together.

Several of the women echoed Lucky's story with tales of "getting in trouble," "playing hooky," fighting at school, and being suspended. For Pam, racism was part of the problem:

> I loved school, but it was like, I had a conduct problem. I had this thing about me being dark. Yeah, it was like they used to call me "overcooked" and um "burnt up." It was kids being kids. Back then when I was in school that was my only problem and I get kicked out, I used to always get kicked out for blaring out, you know? They'd get me angry to the point and I said I can't cry 'cause if I cry they're always going to mess with me. So, I had a very bad conduct problem just because of the color of my skin.

Fine's (1991) research on high school dropouts documented pervasive conduct problems among urban youth. Fine notes that "the relatively heavy rates of suspensions and expulsions which minority youths accumulate nationally combine poorly with the fact that they are less likely to appeal, to have a parent or guardian with the sense of entitlement, knowledge, resources, or strength to challenge successfully" (p. 80).

Although several women were involved in gangs while in high school and skipped school on a regular basis, the majority ultimately dropped out because they got pregnant. Dodson's (1999) research suggests that "many girls leave school first, then become pregnant later, suggesting that they were already detaching from schooling as a pathway to adulthood" (p. 48). For the Project Hope women, although pregnancy often came first, it was still part of the same continuum of experiences:

Yvette: I was pregnant at seventeen, it was rough. You know? I mean, I was having a hard time as it was dealing with the problems that was out there, and then pregnant at seventeen. Then my mother passing away. It really became difficult because I was still at school. So, I mean, the fact that I was pregnant made me stop school for a few months, and the fact that my mother died made me not never wanna go back.

Pam: I had a baby. And at eighteen, I was in eleventh grade. They didn't have what they have for women today. You know what I'm saying? And, the father had start keeping him for a while and I didn't like to come home and my room is destroyed. The baby didn't take a bath, you know. I just couldn't deal with him trying to raise him 'cause he was still using [drugs] and he would take the baby with him over to his other women houses and stuff like that. And I knew the smell on my baby was not a man's smell. It was a woman's smell. So I just said, "I'm gonna stop school and I'll take care of my baby."

As Pam points out when she says "they didn't have what they have for women today," there were few special programs for pregnant teens and teen mothers. Thus, many of the women could not return to school because of lack of child care. Again, Fine (1991) backs up the women's experiences: "Although it is no longer legal to dismiss a student on the basis of her pregnancy or marital status, it is nevertheless commonplace—in fact, typical—for a pregnant teen to drop out because of social pressures, inability to schedule classes, feelings of social rejection, absence of day care, or health problems" (p. 77).

Some women said that they dropped out because of "family problems" (see Fine, 1991; Fine and Zane, 1991; Dodson, 1999). Billie told her story:

> Well the reason why I did drop out was because of my father. My mother left my father with seven children. And I was the second oldest. I had one brother older than me and I was the second oldest, of seven. The rest of 'em were under me, five under me. I wanted to go back to school but I couldn't because there wasn't nobody at home to do things for them. . . . And, you know, my father he was an alcoholic and so forth. And it's just like kinda hard for me 'cause then I had to stay at home and cook and wash clothes and make sure that the other kids got off to school and whatever.

A number of the immigrant women could not attend school in their native countries. For example, in Haiti, the schools had a "tuition fee," which restricted access for the very poor. Winnie, a Haitian immigrant, was forced to do housekeeping work in order to stay with extended family in the United States. Her stepmother deceived her, telling her that she needed to have a green card in order to attend public school in the United States, so she never enrolled.

Leaving school was not an isolated event for the women who ended up in the ALP. Rather, it was part of the fabric of their lives as low-income women of color in America, a fabric also woven out of race, poverty, family relationships, and violence.

Domestic Violence and Isolation

The violence the women experienced in childhood persisted or reappeared in their adult relationships. I found that many of the women do not reveal the violence in their lives to anyone, not even their closest friends. Several expressed these experiences only in their writings. Indeed, it seems likely that the rates of violence are even higher because several women strongly denied being in abusive relationships, although they had visible scars, and the gossip of neighborhood women contradicted their explanations for bruises. A number of these women, such as Jessica, Magdalena, and Delila, repeatedly denied experiences with domestic violence, though I had strong suspicions. For example, Jessica, who had very good attendance, missed school for two weeks because, according to her neighbor Lucky, Jessica's boyfriend had broken into her apartment through the bedroom window and beaten her up. The next day, the Children's Center teachers asked the children to draw pictures of their families, and Jessica's son drew a picture of his mother with a black eye. Jessica was furious that the women were gossiping about her, insisting, "They should just mind their own business." She withdrew her son from the Children's Center and did not return to the Adult Learners Program for two weeks. Jessica is not anomalous: battered women are often afraid and ashamed to disclose incidents of violence (Brandwein, 1999). Another woman, Delila, also repeatedly denied having been battered. When I asked her, she said, "Hey, I'm not the kind of person who stand and get hit." Two women, Soledad and Rachel, were physically assaulted by their teenage sons, but they were ashamed and afraid that if they reported these incidents, the Department of Youth Services (DYS) or the Department of Social Services (DSS) would get involved.

In contrast, Yvette did eventually disclose her abuse and take action against her abuser. Her situation was dire, as she recalls it:

> Aida's father was abusive. He used to lock me up in a room and I used to stay there for five days and four days. And he would bring me the food and he would buy me clothes. He used to give me everything, but I couldn't go outside, I couldn't look out the window. The situation was even worse. I ended up with another kid. That was Lucy. And then when I ended up with my second kid, I was like, oh my God. Where am

> I gonna go? I mean, how is my life gonna be now? I mean, this guy kicks me when I'm pregnant, kicks me in my head, kicks in my stomach. He's pulled guns on my head.

Yvette cried as she told the story: "After a while I said to myself, I can't take this no more. It's either he killing me, or I'm killing him." Finally, she went to the police after her boyfriend bit her face and broke her nose. She said, "I had two big marks bitten in my face and I had black eyes and all that. So I said, well, why not go to the police? This is the best time so they could really see that I'm being abused. So, I went to the police. I got a restraining order on him and I put him in jail. And when I finally put him in jail, I feel so free. I never felt free in my life." Yvette told me she was trying "to fix my life and make up for everything that I done did wrong."

A number of the women stayed in abusive relationships for the sake of their children, and because they wanted their children to have a relationship with their father. The women also worried that the DSS would take their children if they learned about the violence in the home. It was clear that women stayed in abusive relationships because they had few choices. For example, Anna, an undocumented immigrant, lived in constant fear that she would be deported because her son's father, an American citizen, frequently threatened to call the Immigration and Naturalization Service (INS). They had planned to be married, but he had an affair and Anna's paperwork never went through. According to Anna, he took custody of their son and applied for welfare benefits for him. Because she has no legal rights, no income, no housing, and very low literacy skills, she can see her son only when the father "feels like it." Meanwhile, Anna remained homeless for five years, staying with various people she knew through her church.

Unfortunately, during the course of this research I observed that women often left abusive relationships only to return later. In these cases, the women were especially secretive about renewing ties with a batterer for fear of being judged by the other women. It was especially difficult for these women to participate in weekly health classes about domestic violence.

Besides domestic abuse, the violence the women describe includes stories of physical and emotional abuse in schools and while living in the streets. An overwhelming majority of the women who had been assaulted in schools saw this behavior as a fact of life: "people always messing with you." In addition, welfare caseworkers were also often verbally abusive. Each of the women complained about how they were mistreated in welfare offices, and I witnessed these abuses when I accompanied women to their appointments. For example, Elizabeth said she hated welfare because

> The way they talked, treated you, it was like, you were different from everybody else. For whatever reason, they would make it feel like you had a handicap. They treated you like you probably had an arm missing. I mean, you wasn't the good stuff. You was the stuff that you would find on a bargain, instead of the good, nice stuff . . . I'm on clearance. I'm on the clearance rack [laughing]. So they didn't know how to talk. They talk down at you and you know, they're rolling their eyes.

Lisa explained that the hardest thing about being on welfare was how many times she had to go to the welfare offices, "having to go there, having appointments up there, sitting up there at the office all day, and then have to re-certify every couple of months and, ugh, their being in your business about everything, and they want to know. You're the one who's on welfare, and they want to know everything that's going on with everyone else in your house—which is not none of their business. And you tell them that, they get mad and then they mess with you more." This behavior from caseworkers, though not physical violence, compounded the women's senses of themselves as at the mercy of a hostile and dangerous world.

This self-image was in turn exacerbated by a pervasive sense of isolation. When I asked the women, "Who supports you?" in general, many of them say "No one," or "I support myself." Living in a homeless shelter is a last resort for women when their social networks have been exhausted, or are very weak (Liebow, 1993). For example, Tashawna told me, "I feel like I don't have any family and I don't have any friends. You know, and it's hard. I've been making it all my life since I was fifteen years old. I just been depending on Tashawna." Other women had similar experiences and attitudes:

> *Lucky:* I mean, I look at my son and I wake up and I'd be like, "Oh man, I ain't got no money." That's another thing that makes me think, "Oh, let me get this GED." I gotta get a job. I gotta do this. I gotta do that. I need this for my house. I need that for my house. So it's like I motivate myself, you know? I don't have nobody there to push me and be like, "Oh well, you know, Lucky go to school. Lucky get a job. Lucky, do this. Lucky, do that." I've always done everything on my own. I've never went to nobody for money.
>
> *Delila:* I was raised to support myself. Sometimes I have doubt in myself. But it doesn't take me too long to realize it. If it was up to people, I wouldn't be here. If I was the kind of person who depends on people

> who sits there and wishes, to be a millionaire? Well, I'm gonna be sitting there for a long time.

This sense of isolation could be debilitating, but as these quotations show, it also helped motivate the women to take charge of their lives through actions such as enrolling in the ALP.

Many of the women want their children to be as independent as they are. They teach their children, "don't depend on nobody." Billie, who was abandoned by her mother, and Chauntal, whose mother committed suicide, express similar sentiments:

> *Billie:* I always tell Latrice, "There's nobody out there to give you nothing. There's nobody out there to do for you. You got to do and get yourself. You know, don't never depend on nobody. If you depend on anybody, you'll be waiting and waiting and waiting and waiting. So don't depend on nobody. You do what you gotta do to get what you want."
>
> *Chauntal:* With my own kids, I sit down and I talk to my son. I say, "Don't depend on nobody when you get older. Just depend on yourself. Don't think that your sisters and brothers owe you anything because they don't."

It is only slightly ironic that teaching their children independence and survival skills was a primary mode of caring for them.

Homelessness

The issues faced by the Project Hope women culminated in their experiences of homelessness. The intensity of the trauma of homelessness can be seen in the powerful story told to me by Edith, who had been homeless most of her life. Edith's family lived in a car and traveled throughout the southwestern United States for most of her childhood. Then, when she was fourteen years old, her father murdered her mother. She and her siblings were split up among relatives, and she was shuttled back and forth between relatives in New York, New Jersey, and Massachusetts. After all this turmoil, Edith's "greatest desire" is to have a home: "My *dream* is to finally have a beautiful home that my son and I will love. All the places I've lived, I never seem to stay after three years. I want a permanent place that I can live in for years and years without moving so much. That's why I'm working hard to accomplish my goals to get what I want. I feel this is something I will never get, but I want a house badly so I feel I'll get it. That is the only thing I want out of life, if nothing else." Homelessness was a powerful motivating force for these women, but it was also one of their biggest challenges.

Homelessness is a pervasive problem in the Boston area, and it is not going away. As of December 2005, the Boston Homeless Census counted 6,365 homeless individuals, a record 9 percent increase from 2004 (Burge, 2006). The greatest increase in the homeless population was in the number of homeless families, both in shelters and on the street. The total number of family members increased 24 percent, to 2,325 people. There was a 50 percent increase in families staying in shelters or enrolled in transitional programs: a total of 746 households, compared with 505 in 2004 (Burge, 2006). Statewide, at the beginning of January 2004, more than 1,400 families, including 2,800 children, were being sheltered by the DTA each night in their state-funded emergency shelters (Massachusetts Coalition for the Homeless, 2006). It is estimated that twenty thousand Massachusetts children have experienced a housing emergency or actual homelessness (University of Massachusetts, 2000). Between 1995 and 1998, 42 percent of the women enrolled in the ALP were living in homeless shelters (including Project Hope); 58 percent were homeless between 1990 and 1995.

In classes, conversations, and interviews, I learned that, like Edith, many of these women had been homeless several times throughout their childhood and adult lives. The majority of the women became homeless after escaping batterers and unsafe living conditions. The shelter system itself is often inadequate to their needs. According to one study, "Many battered women end up in regular homeless shelters because of inadequate capacity and restricted rules of battered women's shelters"(Roofless Women's Action Research Mobilization [RWARM], 1997, p. 6). These researchers also found that "Many women reported delays and difficulties getting into shelter" because they have to prove that relatives cannot offer them a place to stay (RWARM, 1997, p. 6). According to Boston's Emergency Shelter Commission, the emergency shelter system is "at capacity" and "requests for shelter exceed the number of beds, a situation that continues to endanger the victims of battering and domestic violence" (City of Boston Homeless Census, 2002, p. 13). The state's domestic violence shelters are funded by the Department of Social Services and the family shelters are funded by the Department of Transitional Assistance. These are two separate bureaucratic systems, and battered women often have to "bounce" between them because battered women's shelters are required by the state to have a ninety-day limit (City of Boston Homeless Census, 2002).

Skyrocketing housing costs in the Boston area are another cause of homelessness. One study notes that "43% of families entering shelter identify the homes of relatives or friends as their prior living situation, with 37% coming from a rented home. More and more households in Massachusetts are not able to preserve their tenancies because of increasing housing costs" (University of Massachusetts, 2000, p. 11). During the 1990s the housing market in Boston became extremely tight and affordable-housing shortages developed throughout the state.[1] Many homeless families who could not find low-income housing in the city of Boston were forced to relocate to cities such as Brockton, Lowell, Fall River, and New Bedford. These cities have suffered economically from the exportation of manufacturing jobs, and opportunities for employment remain scarce. At the same time, the city of Boston has been rehabilitated as a desirable place for the upper-middle class, especially young professionals and empty nesters, many of whom are moving in from the suburbs. The rise in rents, combined with the low interest rates of the 1990s, made investing in poorer neighborhoods lucrative and resulted in often-dramatic gentrification.

Because many family shelters are located outside Boston, it is difficult for the women to commute to and from the city. The mothers want their children to remain in the same school and day care, so they use public transportation, which is often unreliable and expensive, to shuttle back and forth from the city to the shelters where they reside. Billie and Delila describe the logistical and financial challenges of living in family shelters outside the Boston area:

> *Billie:* I went to a shelter in Waltham [fifteen miles outside Boston]. And Sharan was in day care and I was commuting back and forth. I had to be at house meetings at 9:30 in the morning. And here I am bringing my kid back and forth to school and it's like no way. And then they would give you points if you was late like for dinner, or for something like that. You had to be there at 5:30 for dinner. I was just like maybe a few minutes, a couple of minutes late, a little after 5:30 and the lady gave me a point. I was like, "Uh-uh. You get ten points, they kicking you out, right?" I'm like, "Oh, no!"
>
> *Delila:* I used to get up at 5 o'clock in the morning, take a shower, wake up my kids, you know, get them ready. I'm out by 7 o'clock to get to Boston. Sometimes, I'm out at 6:30 to get to Boston. I have to be in Boston at 9 o'clock, 8:30. And transportation was very expensive. There's a bus that goes from New Bedford [fifty-eight miles outside of Boston] to South Station. That costs us $5. And then from South Station, I used to take the train to Park Street, the Green Line to Symphony, then, I drop off my kids.

Both women were desperate to return to Boston so they could continue to piece their lives back together. As Delila put it, "I have to go to school. I have to find an apartment. . . . All I need is to get a shelter anywhere near Boston because I wanna continue my school and it would be easier."

However, finding permanent housing is itself a significant challenge, especially given the changes wrought by welfare reform. According to the City of Boston's 2002 homeless census: "The imposition of the two-year time limit for TAFDC, which started in December 1, 1998 impacts many homeless families taking away a source of income that they have relied on to get through hard times. The percentage of Boston homeless families receiving TAFDC has dropped from 71% in 1997 to 49% in 2000. 19% of families in shelter have no income at all" (p. 11). Section 8 is supposed to help low-income families afford housing, but the Boston Housing Authority's Section 8 tenant-based assistance waiting list closed on May 7, 2004. There are currently 4,505 families on the waiting list. Of these families, 95 percent are extremely low income, meaning they earn less than 30 percent of the average median income. The waiting list for Boston Public Housing is even higher, with 10,376 families (Boston Housing Authority, 2006). Across the state, a stunning 49,370 poor families need Section 8 housing subsidies. Of these families on waiting lists statewide, 65.9 percent have children, and another 31.6 percent have members with disabilities (Commonwealth of Massachusetts, Department of Housing and Community Development, 2006).

Even when families "hit the lottery" and obtain the long-awaited and much-coveted Section 8 certificate, the battle is only half won. The women must still find a suitable apartment and a landlord willing to accept the Section 8 certificate—not an easy task, as my field notes about Sylvia's experience demonstrate:

> *October 3, 1997* Sylvia dropped by today and she happily showed me her Section 8 certificate. She was beaming. When Blanche suggested she check out one of the new townhouses being built near Orchard Park, Sylvia immediately said, "Oh, no, I am staying away from Jamaica Plain and Dudley!" She says she will try to find an apartment in Hyde Park, a neighborhood where she can start her life over, a "new beginning."
>
> *March 12, 1998* (Update on Sylvia) Sylvia came by today with bad news. She could not find an apartment, so her Section 8 certificate expired. She waited years for the certificate and it expired because she could not find a place. She says she looked at apartments, but that she felt she was being discriminated against. One "white lady" insisted that Sylvia bring her two-year-old son with her to see the apartment. Sylvia told me, "I'm not stupid. I know what she was trying to do. She wanted to see if my son was hyper." Sylvia felt that indeed if she brought Roberto to the appointment that he would not "sit still" and would "run

> all over the place," thus jeopardizing her chances of getting the apartment. She said, "I guess I'll have to stay with Papo."

In this instance, Sylvia suspected she was denied an apartment because of her son and racism. I observed numerous cases in which a landlord would not rent an apartment to a family with young children because the apartment had not been de-leaded. Boston has some of the nation's oldest housing stock and many old buildings still have lead paint. By not paying for the expenses of de-leading their property, landlords cannot legally rent to families with young children, effectively discriminating against a class of poor parents.

Homelessness was an obstacle for the Project Hope women in numerous dimensions: practically, socially, economically, emotionally. Some factors, such as lead paint, might seem intractable, yet the women were determined to overcome their circumstances. Education was the route they chose.

Going Back to School

Each of the women regretted dropping out of high school:

> *Lucky:* I regret leaving school eight years ago. I woulda had a beautiful job by now. I wouldn't been here. I woulda been out there somewhere.
>
> *Delila:* If I had finished school I would have been in a different place than I am right now. I'm stuck, can't go back and can't go forward. But, I have to make this decision to finish my school and get where I want to go.
>
> *Yvette:* If my mom still would've been alive and all that, I don't think I would've went in the direction I went. I don't think I would've went with Aida's father. I would still stayed home even though I was pregnant. And I think I still would've completed school, you know? I would've finished school and done better now. . . . I would've been in a better predicament than what I am now.
>
> *Billie:* I always wanted to go back to school and I kept that focus. I wanted to go to school. And it was like I didn't really have nobody to encourage me to say, "Oh well you can go back to school, you can do this, you can do that."

The women shared a sense of lost opportunity, and a recognition of the forces that made it difficult for them to stay in school, one of the most important of which was lack of support. Significantly, when the women decided to return to school, they all did so in large part out of a sense of responsibility to others.

The desire to return to school for the sake of their children is a strikingly consistent thread in the writings and educational histories of women in the ALP. Many women return to help their children stay in school:

> *Maxine's writing:* I all way say to my chirdren without an education you can't get no where. Then one day my daughter came home and said to me, mommy you allways tell us to go to school and get an education. But look at you. You are not doing nothing for yourself but sitting home everyday telling us we should do this or that you can't tell us nothing! You do what you need to do for yourself, then you can preach to us. So that's why I'm back in school because she was write.
>
> *Renata:* I decided to go back to school so I could be a good role model for my kids. I say that because how can I teach them something, or tell them something I don't know? How can I tell my kids to go to, or finish school, if I didn't? They'll be looking at me saying, "Why should I go to school you didn't finish.". . . And, I'm really glad I decided to come back. Now I can get to where I want to be for me and my kids.

For others, economic advancement for themselves and their children is a crucial motivating factor:

> *Margarita's writing:* I decide to go back to school not only for myself but for my baby. I feel if I go back to school get my GED and find myself a good job or get into a training my daughter and I would be living lovely, but right now we're not. We are struggling for every little thing we got and its hard. I would go a day or to without eating just so she could have a little something to eat except milk all the time.

As Lucky put it, "I need this certificate for myself, for my son, to get higher education . . . to get a good job."

In focusing on their children, the women embody the "mothering discourses" that frequently dominate discussions of women's literacy. In chapter 1, I explained how proponents often frame their arguments in favor of adult literacy education by arguing that literacy is "good for the economy" (National Institute for Literacy, 1998). However, the rhetoric of adult literacy shifts when it specifically addresses women: according to Smythe and Isserlis (2003), "institutions that promote family literacy policies and programs, such as schools, government education departments and welfare agencies, are shaped by *mothering discourses:* culturally bound beliefs and values that form society's definition of good mothers, normal families, and, by extension, appropriate literacy and parenting practices in the home" (p. 25, italics in original).[2]

Smythe and Isserlis studied family literacy texts and found three types of mothering discourses: the discourse of "the normal family," which "privileges the two-parent, heterosexual, nuclear family where women occupy the domestic sphere of child-raising and men occupy the public sphere of work outside the home" (p. 26); the "discourse of mothering as pedagogy," which positions the mother as "their child's first and most important teacher" (p. 26); and the "discourse of maternal responsibility," which holds that "if women are natural teachers, they are also naturally responsible for the educational outcomes of their children. This is reinforced in the doctrines of personal responsibility that underlie parental involvement policies in No Child Left Behind, as well as in other texts and advice that link children's literacy and schooling success to mothering" (p. 28). Carmack (1992) (see also Auerbach 1989) critiques the goals of family literacy programs, for they "focus on mothers teaching children to read and write in order to break the cycle of illiteracy. In so doing, the programs subordinate the importance for women of literacy skills as a way out of confining roles and relationships within the family and society" (p. 180).[3] Luttrell's (2003) research discusses these issues within the context of schooling for pregnant girls. Luttrell describes "the education as a responsibility approach, whether related to pregnancy or motherhood or sexuality, frames educational conflicts and decisions in terms that may limit a girl's sense of self-regard and importance. 'If you are not going to do it for yourself, then at least do it for your child'" (p. 23).

As seen above and throughout this study, the Project Hope women's motivations to participate in literacy classes and their beliefs about education are shaped by these hegemonic discourses about mothering and motherhood. The women internalize the neoliberal ideology of personal responsibility for themselves and their children. If their children fail in school, it is because they have failed as mothers (just as their mothers failed them), so they go back to school to be more responsible, to be good role models, and to help their children succeed in school. Yet while the dominant "mothering discourses" are clearly important motivating factors for the women, they also prove quite contradictory for "welfare mothers." As I will show later, because of work-first policies, many of the women had to give up on their educations and work in low-paying jobs.

The motivations of the Project Hope women are consistent with Wikelund's (1993) research, as well as Dowdy's (2003) study of black women who participate in GED programs. Wikelund studied twenty-seven welfare recipients who were required to participate in "Career and Life Planning" and "Pathways to Progress" programs. Although these welfare mothers were mandated to enroll in these educational programs—otherwise they risked losing their welfare benefits—Wikelund found that the women were motivated to attend because of concrete basic needs, as well as "individual and symbolic motives" (p. 27). For example, the women in the study were motivated to participate in adult education because they needed "income for basic survival," they were concerned with their "children's well-being," they wanted "better jobs," they wanted "independence," they wanted to be "good role models for their children," and they wanted to be "doing something for themselves" (pp. 27–28). Dowdy found several themes in the stories of why black women returned to school for their GEDs. These themes included: an "inner drive to improve each woman's circumstances" (p. 48), children as a motivating factor, "ambition for a better life," the belief that "school was a necessary step" to achieving dreams (p. 51), and the perception that the GED was necessary for obtaining good jobs. Beder's and Valentine's (1990) research similarly suggests "10 basic motivations" for adults attending adult education classes: "self-improvement, family responsibilities, diversion, literacy development, community/church involvement, job advancement, launching, economic need, educational advancement, and urging of others" (quoted in Wikelund, 1993, p. 28). Like the subjects of these studies, the Project Hope women returned to school for a nexus of reasons, though their children were always a primary factor.

Fifteen Project Hope women were required by the Department of Transitional Assistance (DTA), the Department of Social Services (DSS), or the shelter where they were residing, to enroll in an educational activity. Although these women were required to participate in educational activities, they still said that they were going to school for their children and to "better myself." Tashawna explains why she returned to school: "Well to tell the truth, I got a letter in the mail from my welfare worker. But that really had nothing to do with it. I mean, it had something to do with it, but I always wanted to go to school. I always wanted to learn. You know? It's just in me, you know . . . I mean, it has something to do with welfare, but it really didn't because I always wanted to go to school. As you can see all the schools that I been through."

The immigrant women who enroll at Project Hope express many of the same reasons for returning to school as their native-born classmates, such as increased economic opportunities, but their desire to learn English is also a motivating factor. For example, Helena writes, "Today I feel very greatful to take the opportunity to talk about why I decide to come back to school. First, I want to speak English fluently so I can do something better in the future. I realize I have to spend sometimes in school learn how to write read and speak properly. Second, I think when somebody do a studie of anything you feel comfortable with, you will be able to move easily with the goal you wish to reach in your life."

For a number of women, the fact that their own mothers did not have a formal education inspired them to be role models for their own children. In their education histories, the women were asked to talk about the messages they received from their families about education. A number of women, such as Tashawna, would be the first in their families to graduate with a high school diploma, "My mother had eleven children. And not one of my sisters or brothers had finished school. I'm the only one that has always been back to this school and that school, and this school and that school. I've always constantly went back. Tried to go back." Billie's younger siblings obtained their high school diplomas, and it is her turn now:

> My younger sister, she finished school. My brother Rodney, he finished school. And I think my sister Shari got her GED. And see these are all the kids that's under me. They got their high school, they finished school or either got their GED. So I'm like saying to myself, I know I can do this. And I'm still saying, I can do this and I'm gonna do it. I'm gonna do it. Long as I keep up, long as I know what I have to do, I'm gonna go on and do it. You know, 'cause before I know it, I'll be forty years old and it's just in two more years. I mean, before the year's over if I turn forty years old, I'm gonna accomplish my goal. That's to get my high school diploma, get training, take up some type of training course and then go to college and go do two years of college, or whatever to get some type of degree or whatever. I'm not getting no younger, you know? I got to do something because my daughter be eighteen. She's going into her last year of school. So she got one more year. She only has one cousin that's older than her. It's her, my nephew, and then her. They're the two oldest and all the rest of 'em are younger than her. So she told my mother, "I'm gonna be the first one of your grandkids to finish high school." And I said, "That's good."

Luttrell's (1997) research on working-class women who enroll in adult literacy classes found that a number of the women expressed resentment toward their mothers, attributing their "school failures" to their mothers. Luttrell writes, "I maintain that one of the reasons the women's school stories are told with so much passion is because they harbor unresolved feelings towards mothers whom they, at times consciously and at other times unconsciously, hold accountable for what society and school have denied them" (p. 10). A few Project Hope women certainly felt this way. For example, Mahogany was still resentful toward her mother, and she wanted to do things differently:

> When I had my daughter I decided that things were different, I needed to make things different and do things different than how my mother did them. So I decided that I needed to go back to school and finish my education because, I didn't want her to ask me a question and I couldn't answer it, you know? And I wanted my daughter always to be able to come to me first, instead of asking someone else, someone in the street, or something. So that was a really big thing for me at that time in my life, to make sure that *I* was there for her, the way my mother wasn't there for me.

When I asked Mahogany if her mother was happy that she completed her GED, she told me: "As far as my mother ever know about that, I don't know if she even know that I graduated. She never asked. After a while she know I was in the program, but she never said to me, "Did you get your GED?" Another woman, Angela, described how her mother did not support her decision to go back to school. Angela told me: "My mother was like, 'What? What are you going to go in there for? Just so you won't pass, so you won't do anything?' That's what my mother told me. 'You're not going to do it, why are you go over there?'" When I asked her, "Was there anybody that gave you support?" Angela said, "I mean, my friends, my friends. But my mother was like, 'Why are you going to go in there? So you won't do it?'"

Delila complained that "I see a lot of parents that are just like my mother, who don't know what school is and how important it is for the children's future. They just let their children screw up their life and they just sit home and don't do nothing about it." Delila's comments display the hegemonic notion that some women do not value education and "let their children screw up their life." Other women, such as Pam, expressed sympathy with their mothers, understanding their shared problems and challenges:

> My mother's father died when they was young. My mother was ten or eleven and she had eleven brothers and sisters. And my mother's one of the older ones. And my uncle, and my aunt, my mother all three of them dropped out of school about the same grade. . . . I was talking to her about coming to school the other day and she's scared. I said, "Ma, why don't you come to my school?" Cause she said she's tired of sitting in the house. And you know her legs, her knees be bothering her now. Cause they said when she used to be younger she'd kneeled down on the ground and pick the cotton, she caught coal up in her. But she didn't know it was coal up in her. So she's afraid to come to school. And I've been talking to her, trying to get her to come here. I was telling her, "Ma, come on!" She said, "Well, I dropped out, I'm not gonna know anything." She's afraid that she's not gonna know anything. And tears start drop-

> ping, she had me crying. I'm like "Ma, just come and try it." You know what I'm saying? "They'll help you, trust me." She's just afraid. That's an experience she had. She told me that she didn't want to stop going to school. But she said she got pregnant.

Pam's mother's missed educational opportunities appear to serve as a motivating factor for her to complete her own education.

Their mothers were not the only figures in the women's lives ambivalent about their educational ambitions. When women enroll in the ALP, they believe they are making a positive change in their lives, but sometimes their peers and the men in their lives do not want them to change, and present additional obstacles to the women's goals. This is confirmed in several studies of adult learners (Fingeret, 1983; Rockhill, 1990; Dowdy, 2003). According to Dowdy (2003):

> Network patterns shift once a student enrolls in a class to increase his or her literacy skills. The student's strong commitment to learn in the face of the challenge of a new or crumbling network system can create a source of tremendous discomfort among group members. Because of this change in the social network pattern and the kinds of support activities that the group traditionally provided for itself, it is clear that the decision of the literacy student to venture out in the world and to be exposed to experiences otherwise unavailable to the rest of the network is a considerable challenge to the status quo of the group. (p. 5; also see Rockhill, 1990)

Illustrating this analysis, Elizabeth describes how her boyfriend was supportive when she began classes, but later changed:

> My son's father, he was there towards the beginning, but he figured I wasn't going to do it. When he seen I was doing it, when I actually went to take the tests and I started passing, then he started to get like, "Hmm." And then he started making things kind of hard for me. And that's when with the Saturday mornings of going to take the test—he made it so hard. He didn't want to take me, he made it so difficult, so hard . . . when I graduated and, you all gave us the nice graduation ceremony . . . my son's father, who I looked to come, he didn't come.

Boyfriends were not the only social impediments. The women in the ALP perceive themselves to be changing women and they believe that some people do not want them to change. Tashawna stated it explicitly: "Everybody used to want to come over on Mondays and Tuesdays, and Wednesdays, because they didn't want me to change. They didn't like the change. But now they have no choice, because I don't have nothing in my way anymore. So now, they are all just scattered everywhere. They disappeared on me." Pam describes how the women in her community were particularly resistant:

> If someone said, "Why don't you get a job, Why you going to school?" You should see the way I act. I say "Oh no! Nuh, uh. I did it before, I ain't gonna do it again. No, I'm going to school. When I'm finished with school then I get a job!" Other than that, I'm staying right in the schoolhouse where I am at." "Well, you ain't going fast enough!" "Listen, no!" My mother always calls me and says, "Girl, you hold your head up high, and act like you don't hear it." Cause there's a lot of women that be around you that tell you, "Why don't you get a job?" Or, "Why you going to this school and you not achieving nothing?" But they don't know what I am achieving, because I don't speak to them on that level. What you do during the day is what you do, what I do during the day is what I do. And you have a lot of women that always be . . . I don't think they're always against you, but I think they have their little say-so about things. Like in the morning when sometimes I leave, they say, "Girl, all you do is go to school!" They be out in the morning hanging out in the street. They be hanging in the street. And I come out, you know, prep up the car, have the kids ready with me, or take them to the bus stop. And you always hear, "Why you?" . . . First of all they have a beef about the way you dress, number one. Then number two, they got a beef about "Why you go to school?" Why!? Because you ain't going nowhere without an education!

Although Pam was fortunate to have the support of her mother, Elizabeth was less lucky. However, she pointed to a crucial source of support for all the women: their peers in the ALP. "My family, when they did come, they really wasn't too much, as happy as I had expected them to be. But I really had my main support with the people, the women I went to school with. They were my backbone, they supported me, and if it wasn't for them, and my teachers, I wouldn't have did it."

Conclusion

This chapter has detailed the life experiences of the Project Hope women. Though violence and abuse, teen pregnancy, dropping out of school, and homelessness were shared obstacles, the women also shared a determination to improve their lives, and, as Elizabeth notes, they shared the challenge of succeeding in the Adult Learners Program, a challenge made that much easier by the fact that it was shared. The Project Hope women were themselves involved in helping make the Adult Learners Program's structure and curriculum more responsive to the needs of the learners. In a focus group with Sister Lois, several women discussed ways to support new students and ideas for the orientation of new women:

Pam: I think when you interview them, you should ask them what kind of experience they had in school.

Tashawna: Right.

Pam: So you can find out if this is the correct program for them.

Tashawna: Right.

Pam: 'Cause I see a lot of women coming in and just dropping out and I'm like [shrugs her shoulders] . . .

Lorna: Why do you think that happens?

Pam: Because, you have to ask them, "What was your experience in school? How come you didn't finish, or how come you're here? What brought you here?" 'Cause you need a solid thing for yourself because some people come here because you're made to come here.

Tashawna: Right.

Pam: You got to want to be here to come and keep coming. You got to want something for yourself.

Tashawna: Or I think Sister Lois should, just like you said, after she gets finished saying everything you had just spoke upon, I think Sister Lois should ask the person, "Do they have any obstacles in their way right now that's gonna keep them from continuing on with the program through?"

Pam: Yup! Sometimes the obstacles—they don't see 'em. Sometimes we don't see what's coming at us.

Tashawna: Right.

Lucky: That's true.

Pam: We could talk to them like, "Why are you here? What are your goals? What are you gonna do afterwards?"

The women's growing sense of commonality and responsibility toward other women like themselves is evident in this exchange, which itself exemplifies the value of the ALP's popular education approach. Tashawna's and Pam's understanding of how obstacles interfere with school is informed by their own experiences in the program, and in turn they use those experiences to help improve conditions for other women. The next chapter describes the educational programs in the ALP, and how they directly drew upon and responded to the participants' lives.

294 Bowdoin ST.
Joseph
Ivy Smith
welfare.
Joanne you are cutoff go do some worcfare and bring me back some of your mony since I pay your taxes
well back to the welfare to see what happens I hope Ms. Joseph don't cut me off

4 *Around the Round Table*

> We met around a round table, connected, it seemed, only by our gender and the table surface. We were varying shades of black, brown, white. We were from the rural South, the urban North, suburban Midwest, the islands, Puerto Rico. Our differences were apparent.
>
> But over the weeks, around the round table, we began to throw back and forth a shuttle of words. The threads came first from the works of Alice Walker, Maya Angelou, Isabel Allende, Robert Frost; then we began to appropriate their words to our own experience. Tentatively, at first, we wove a pattern of connectedness around and across our round table.
>
> We began to put on the table the threads of deeper hues, those that glowed with childhood agony, teenage anger, adult despair—tentatively at first, but with greater confidence as the weeks wore on that the cloth we were weaving together could contain all these. And we found that, in sharing, the cloth became stronger, around and across our round table we found a common language of struggle, and a common passion for liberating truth.
>
> —Robin, a teacher in the Adult Learners Program

Cultures of Silence

The pedagogy and curriculum of the Adult Learners Program at Project Hope builds upon the work of major twentieth-century figures in popular education. Gramsci (1971) argued that indoctrination through the educational curriculum and its institutions (rather than force) is the means by which the modern state ensures a shared hegemony (or consensus) of aspirations and beliefs.[1] Gramsci explained how dominant ideas are supported through the consent of the dominated groups, and he analyzed the role that the dominated play in their own oppression. According to Aronowitz and Giroux (1993), understanding hegemony can offer insight into "the constant structuring of consciousness as well as a battle for the control of consciousness" (p. 83). McLaren (1998) explains how hegemony works:

> Hegemony is not a process of active domination as much as an active structuring of the culture and experiences of the subordinate class by the dominant class. The dominant culture is able to "frame" the ways in which subordinate groups live and respond to their own cultural system and lived experiences; in other words, the dominant culture is able to manufacture dreams and desires for both dominant and subordinate groups by supplying "terms of reference" (i.e., images, visions, stories, ideals) against which all individuals are expected to live their lives. The dominant culture tries to "fix" the meaning of signs, symbols, and representations to provide a "common" worldview, disguising relations of power and privilege through organs of mass media and state apparatus such as schools, government institutions, and state bureaucracies. (p. 183)

Popular education, by contrast, helps individuals, especially individuals from subordinate groups, to challenge those "signs, symbols, and representations."

Gramsci's (1971) work on hegemony and "contradictory consciousness" provides a critical theoretical frame for understanding the work of Brazilian philosopher Paulo Freire. Freire's literacy work with peasants and workers in developing nations influenced educational programs throughout the world, including the Adult Learners Program (Gadotti, 1994). Freire was critical of mainstream teaching practices, referring to them as "banking education." According to Freire, in the banking approach to education, the teacher "deposits" information into an "empty account" (the student) who "receives, memorizes, and repeats" (1990, p. 58). The educator is the subject of the educational process while the students are the objects. The teacher knows; the students do not know. The teacher (or school system) chooses the content of the curriculum; the students do not have input.

A number of research studies in the past decade examine how banking education in schools mirrors social stratification in society. For example, Anyon's (1997) research comparing classrooms in different socioeconomic communities highlighted class-based distinctions in curriculum content and instruction. Anyon and other researchers concluded that instruction in inner-city and poor schools often centers around unchallenging, low-level work, with an emphasis on rote material. In Polakow's (1993) research with "at-risk" students, she found that the major indicators of success for low-income students were obedience and compliance to routinized tasks, and "there was a pervasive ethos of containment and regulation—drilling children to produce correct responses, regulating their imagination, presenting them with tasks to be completed rather than learning encounters" (p. 150). Polakow argues that poor children are rarely "given extra doses of talk-time, of expressive activities, of discovery-oriented projects that they themselves control. Lacking autonomy in almost every part of their world, they are further denied it in school. Thinking, imagining, inventing, hands-on learning threaten to subvert the order of what Foucault has termed the discipline of docile bodies, the structuring of a child's consciousness and the vitiation of expressive possibilities" (p. 157).

Freire argues that banking education aims to maintain the division between those who know and those who do not, that is, the division between the oppressor and the oppressed. Banking approaches to education deny people the opportunity to "become more fully human" and to fully develop their potential (Freire, 1990). According to Freire, the student-as-object is submerged in a "culture of silence" that results in feelings of powerlessness and an inability to change one's life circumstances. In contrast, Freire offers a vision of an educational process that is dialogic, empowering, and transformative:

> [T]o exist, humanly, is to *name* the world, to change it. . . . If it is in speaking their world that men, by naming the world, transform it, dialogue imposes itself as the way in which men achieve significance as men. Dialogue is thus an existential necessity. And since dialogue is the encounter in which the united reflection and action of the dialoguers are addressed to the world which is to be transformed and humanized, this dialogue cannot be reduced to the act of one person's "depositing" ideas in another, nor can it become a simple exchange of ideas to be "consumed" by the discussants. (1990, p. 77, italics in original)

Freire also suggests that in order to break through the "cultures of silence," the issues discussed in educational activities must be close to the daily lives and reality of the participants.

As I explained in chapter 2, the founding teachers at Project Hope were Catholic sisters. From the beginning, they used Catholic social teaching methods and popular education approaches. In 1961, the Catholic Church in Brazil sponsored a national literacy program based on Freire's literacy work (Freire, 1973; Gadotti, 1994; Ferreira and Ferreira, 1997).[2] According to Ferreira and Ferreira (1997),

> One of the most active movements [in Brazil] was the Catholic Action group, made up mainly of Catholic University students and the Young Catholic Workers organization. Catholic Action developed a uniquely efficient method of analysis to understand their reality, and action to transform this reality. Their method was based on three steps: *Ver*—TO SEE, *Julgar*—TO JUDGE, *Agir*—TO ACT. In practice this meant: 1) To see the situation lived by participants; 2) To judge (or analyze) this situation at its root causes, including its particular socio-economic, political, cultural aspects; 3) To act, to change this situation, following the precepts of social justice. (p. 18)

This approach, referred to as the "Catholic Action Method," was used in a variety of settings, especially in teaching literacy to poor workers. According to Torres (1995), popular education projects

> arise from a political and social analysis of the living conditions of the poor and their outstanding problems (such as unemployment, malnourishment, poor health) and attempt to engage the poor in individual and collective awareness of those conditions. Second, they base their educational practice on collective and individual previous experiences (as previous knowledge), and they work in groups rather than on an individual basis. Third, the notion of education provided by these projects is related to the concrete skills or abilities that they try to instill in the poor . . . and these projects strive to arouse self-reliance among participants. (p. 243)

In the United States, such popular education programs are more likely to be offered in community-based organizations (CBOs) than in organizations funded by federal or state governments (Beder, 1996). Government and for-profit organizations are more likely to reflect the interests of those in power and operate in a "top-down" manner. But at CBOs such as Project Hope, we find an approach to education that is compatible with, indeed, deeply influenced by, the popular education philosophy: "education that serves the interests of the popular classes (exploited sectors of society), that involves them in critically analyzing their social situation and organizing to act collectively to change the oppressive conditions of their lives" (Beder, 1996, p. 74).

At Project Hope, this approach was embodied in the use of *generative themes* and *codes.* As I noted above, Freire believed that educational activities need to be rooted in the issues that affect participants' lives. Freire refers to these issues as generative themes:

> In order to communicate effectively, educator and politician must understand the structural conditions in which the thought and language of the people are dialectically framed. It is to the reality which mediates men,

> and to the perception of that reality held by educators and people, that we must go to find the program content of education. The investigation of what I have termed the people's "thematic universe"—the complex of their "generative themes"—inaugurates the dialogue of education as the practice of freedom . . . consistent with the liberating purpose of dialogical education, the object of the investigation is not men (as if men were anatomical fragments), but rather the thought-language with which men refer to reality, the levels at which they perceive that reality, and their view of the world, in which their generative themes are found. (1990, p. 86)

To find generative themes, the teacher learns from students about the issues that mean the most to them. Once these generative themes are found, they become the basis for discussion, reflection, and action (Schnapp, 1998). Freire's popular education work was conducted in "Culture Circles," discussion groups in which the educators and learners used codes to engage in dialogue about their generative themes. A code is a representation of the learner's day-to-day situation. It can be an object, a photograph, a drawing, a poem, a film, a skit, or even a word. The code enables theoretical abstractions about the concrete reality it represents: "The purpose of a code is to represent a generative theme to the learners so that they can clearly see the issue or problem, emotionally respond to it, critically reflect on it, and take action in regards to it" (Association for Community-Based Education, 1988, p. 24). The goal of popular education is the development of "conscientization," a critical consciousness, or, as Freire understood it, "the never-ending process by which man takes on his position as a creature of praxis, in transforming and humanizing the world" (Andreola, 1993, p. 229).

The generative themes at Project Hope were largely related to the women's experiences as low-income, homeless, and formerly homeless women of color and, especially, as mothers. As we will see in this chapter, topics such as school (their own and their children's), parenting, African American history, and welfare reform were effective generative themes. For codes, the teachers and the women used homeless women's writings, newspaper articles, editorial cartoons, music, pictures, videos, short skits, and the like.

The Catholic Action group's principles—TO SEE, TO JUDGE, TO ACT—helped shape how the teachers and women at the ALP used generative themes and codes. In discussions, the women described "What" they understood or thought about the problems or issues represented in a code (TO SEE). They discussed what was happening in the code, and whether they had experienced the circumstances and problems it represented. Group discussion (dialogue) and writing also facilitated critical reflection about the generative themes (TO JUDGE). For example, the women talked about "Why" or "How" the problems existed, what the history and causes of the problems were, and what could be done to address them. The endpoint of the process was often taking action in response to the solutions or strategies discussed, and then reflecting on that action, again, in discussions and in writing (TO ACT). The women would identify what they could do on a personal level to address the problems represented in the codes. They also discussed what they could do together, as a group of women with shared interests, immediately and in the long term, to solve the underlying causes of their problems. In the next sections, I explore this educational process through portraits of popular education classrooms at Project Hope. I look specifically at how a pedagogy based on generative themes and codes was enacted in "Women & Society," Economic Literacy, Participatory Health Literacy, and "Loves Herself. Regardless" classes.

Banking and Popular Education Approaches

When I began teaching at Project Hope, I discovered how invested I was in the banking approach to education. I was team-teaching an "American History" class with Robin Jones, an experienced popular education teacher. Having observed Robin's teaching, I decided to begin class by using the Bill of Rights as a code for a discussion about the United States Constitution. I began the class by asking a series of questions about the Bill of Rights that I had developed in advance. As I stood in front of the women, who were seated in a circle, I asked them: "What are the first ten amendments to the Constitution called? What are the three branches of the U.S. government? What are the five freedoms protected by the first amendment?" After I asked about a dozen questions, I faced silence, blank stares, and sighs of frustration. Crystal suddenly asked me, "Who was the first black man in the White House?" I said, "Well, there were slaves in the White House, our first presidents had slaves." This answer clearly frustrated her. Then she proudly announced that the first black person in the White House was "Booker T. Washington." She had switched the topic of discussion from the Bill of Rights to black history, a topic she seemed to know more about and that was more interesting to her.

While I attempted to guide the class back to the Constitution (the topic we were supposed to be discussing), Crystal interrupted with yet another question: "What was the first black newspaper?" The other women were really interested in Crystal's questions and looked at me expectantly, believing that as the teacher I would have the right answer. I did not know. Pam quickly said, "I know the answer! *The Final Call.*" I told the women that I did not know the answer, but that it was probably not *The Final Call* (the Nation of Islam's newspaper). I still felt pressured to direct the discussion back to what they needed to know for the GED, but the women wanted to learn more about African Americans in history, a topic that would not be covered on the social studies GED test.

Crystal and the other women were frustrated with my banking approach to teaching history. I had selected the topic for discussion without attempting to connect the issues more directly to the women's experiences. I had also asked a series of closed-end questions rather than open-ended questions. This authoritarian approach made Crystal and the other women feel dumb and ashamed. Robin, who had been observing this class, said, "Why don't we take a few minutes to think about any questions we have about the U.S. Constitution? Let's write these down on a piece of paper. We'll try to find the answers together." Using a popular education process, Robin was able to lead us back to the topic we needed to cover. Rather than posing questions to them, encouraging the women to talk about the questions they have enables teachers and learners to create knowledge together, through sharing what they know and what they want to learn, and then searching for answers together. When popular education begins with the questions and experiences of the learners, it fosters meaningful dialogue based on common interests that can lead to transformative learning.

Popular education approaches use relevant and meaningful materials to teach literacy skills (Auerbach, 1992). I observed that many of the women became excited about learning when the subject matter taught them something about themselves, their children, and their community. For example, Delila told me, "If I am learning, if there is a subject that interests me, I don't get bored. But, if there is a subject that's gonna be boring, I can get sleepy. I just get distracted so easily. I'll find ways to let my mind go easy. So that's the problem with me. We need something that's going to interest us, something that's going to involve us. Not something we have to do because we were told to do it." An example of the kind of engaging learning experience that women such as Delila yearned for is the book Project Hope teachers publish every year containing the writings of the homeless women in the ALP. These books become reading material and written codes for other learners. The women's writings are also shared with other adult literacy programs and copies are deposited in the Boston Public Library.

In the fall of 2004, I interviewed Mahogany, who told me that the first book project was her idea. She told me: "I'm the one who came up with the idea about we need to put all this stuff in a book 'cause it's just amazing, you know?" She convinced Robin, who said, "You know what, that's a good idea." Mahogany explained: "We needed to talk to everybody to see if they, how they wanted to do that. So my idea was to have everybody write a little story about, a little piece about their life, going from present to future. That's how it was supposed to be. What they went through, what they're going through now, and what they think they're going to be later. That's how the format was going to be. I wrote mine in five seconds." The other women in the group were more reluctant to write about their experiences, so Mahogany shared her story about being raped when she was nine years old. In her account of what happened next, Mahogany reveals the core methodologies of popular education:

> I was like, let me read mine out, let me see what you all think about it. I read mine out, boom-boom, and everybody's mouth was like, "You put all that personal stuff in there?" I said, "I need to put it on paper, I write everything on paper." And who better to share it with than a whole bunch of women? We all went through the same thing; it's no secret. You know. And everybody was like, with tears in their eyes, like, "Mahogany, I can't believe you put that on paper. I would have never thought to put that on paper. That's so personal." Well, we said we were going to put it in a book, let's be real about it. After that, everybody said, "I need a new piece of paper!" After that, that's when the whole book got like crazy, because everybody was like, Oh my God, let me put this down. . . . And it was like really, really deep and, and got down to then it turned into a lesson, because it turned in from the book, from writing what your thoughts were to re-writing it, to putting the proper words in it, to punctuation, to how to put it on the paper, how to type it, you know. It was like it went into a big lesson, which was good for the English teacher, because then it got us back on what we need to learn to write a letter for work, or uh, um, a resume, or, you know? Those things. And come to find out, 90 percent of them didn't know how to write a letter, 90 percent of them didn't know how to do word processing, or stop putting and, and, and. They just used dictionaries and made us look up what else some words meant another way, which came into a lesson. Which means that, like I said, you need personal and you need school to make it work for older people who's already been halfway through life. 'Cause it makes it more like they're not being punished for not doing something that they should have done. You see what I'm trying to say?

This was a paradigmatic example of how generative themes foster learning: the women shared their stories with the group, discovered their shared experiences, wrote about topics that mattered deeply to their own lives, and then used that writing to build skills.

Motherhood and Parenting

"Motherhood and Parenting" were common generative themes in Project Hope's popular education classes because the women struggled to provide for their children, and they often placed their children's needs ahead of their own. Like many of the women, Delila said, "All I have is my children." I observed strong emotional ties between the homeless mothers and their children. This is consistent with other research studies that have found strong emotional bonds between a single mother and her child (Bassuk, 1990; Dail, 1990).

The writings of low-income mothers were used to elicit generative themes. For example, the following paragraph written by Soledad, a thirty-four-year-old mother of four, served as a "code" for a writing class:

> One time I was at the bus station waiting for the bus. I kept hearing a little boy crying and I was asking myself, "Why is the little boy crying?" So, I decided to walk over to see why he was crying. The reason that the little boy was crying was because his mother kept yelling at him and spanking him because he did not wanted to sit down. And, then, everybody started staring at her and she came out and said, "What the hell you all looking at!? This is my child and I do whatever I want to do. So stop fucking staring at me and mine your business!"

Soledad's story raised many issues for the mothers in a writing class I observed. After Soledad read the story aloud, all of the mothers said that they could relate to the frustrated mother at the bus stop. When asked to describe what the problem was, Elizabeth said, "The mother is stressed out." Adrienne agreed and added that people are always "getting in your business." The women then discussed whether Soledad should have said something to the "stressed out" mother. Angela said that she had seen bruises on a little boy who was friends with her son. She wanted to call the DSS, and Elizabeth encouraged her to do so. Then, Diva quickly said, "But I don't think you should call DSS, you never know what that family is going through." Diva's own son was in DSS custody, though the other women in the class did not know this.

Many of the women expressed a deep fear of losing custody of their children. They worried that disputes with other people might result in a false report of child abuse to the Department of Social Services (DSS), or they feared that if they filed restraining orders against boyfriends, DSS would be notified by the courts. Twelve women had children who were in DSS custody and five had children who were in the custody of the Department of Youth Services (DYS). These women had to attend parenting classes and group counseling and, in a few cases, be enrolled in an educational activity before they could regain custody of their children.

DSS was a significant source of anxiety for these women. As welfare recipients living in shelters, their parenting practices were under special scrutiny (Haig-Friedman, 2000). I observed women who would not let their children speak while in the presence of an authority figure such as a shelter case manager, or welfare caseworker. It was understandable that the women would try to silence their children in front of authorities; after all, these authorities had the power to take custody of their children, if they judged them to be unfit mothers.

The discussion regarding Soledad's story evolved into a general discussion about hitting children. Diane, the teacher, asked, "How and when does one discipline children? Was it okay for the mother at the bus stop to hit her child because the child wouldn't sit down?" Denise replied, "Well, it depends on how hard she hit him. My son doesn't sit still, so I have to hit him sometimes." Jessica, who is Puerto Rican, suggested that there are cultural differences about disciplining children. She said that her mother used to beat her and her sister with an extension cord, a slipper, or any other object she could find during her fits of anger. She said, "Puerto Rican mothers are no joke. I guess me and my sister deserved it for disrespecting her. Maybe if some nosy person saw my mother hitting us, they woulda put us in foster care. But I don't think it was abuse, like how they say it is today."

As the women continued to share stories about how they were hit as children, they were quite animated and began talking at the same time. I observed how Diane tried to guide them toward a discussion about the roots of violence. She asked, "Why is there violence in our society? And, what can we do to stop violence?" Denise, who had not spoken much, suggested that television perpetuated violence. Adrienne argued that people should "talk about things like human beings, instead of fighting." As time ran out, the group decided that the topic of the next writing assignment would be, "If someone hit your child in school, what would you do?"

At the next class, while the women read aloud their essays about what they would do if their child was hit in school, discussion was lively. Adrienne said she would talk to her child's teacher first, then the principal, and if necessary, the parents of the other child. Pam and Lisa argued that "the world is violent" and people need to protect themselves. Elizabeth insisted that "violence breeds violence." The majority of the women said that they would not encourage their children to fight back. In an interview with me later, Pam expressed her disagreement with her classmates, saying, "I'm quick to fight. Some of 'em ain't quick to fight. They quick to talk it out." She explained:

> We wrote this article about the kids. If somebody hit your kid in school, what would you do? . . . I told them I ain't teaching my kid not to hit back. You know what I'm saying? And a lot, most of the women said they would. Only me and Lisa agreed. But see, Lisa had to go through similar beat ups and stuff like that. Some of these women probably ain't got, never got beat up or jumped, or they didn't have the same lifestyle I had. I don't teach my kids to go out there and fight with guns and knives. But if somebody hits them, I tell them to hit 'em back.

These issues were so pedagogically effective because they related directly to the women's lives. As Pam described "beat ups," Angela was dealing with exactly the topic the women had written about. Her daughter was having problems in school and her teacher had called that morning. "[My daughter's teacher] called today to tell me that some boy hit her and she hit the boy back. And I was like, "Well, if he hit her first, obviously she's going to hit him back." I said, "I have no problem with her hitting nobody back, if they hit her first." And I left it alone like that. Honestly, because she's tiny and otherwise, you know what I mean. . . ." The classroom discussion enabled the women to gain critical perspective on issues they faced every day, and to articulate their perspectives in writing.

The generative themes of "Motherhood and Parenting" in popular education classes also highlighted internalized gender oppression in the form of the prejudice the women had against each other. For example, a few women actually said they "hated" other women. One woman, Georgia, who initially misunderstood the mission of the Adult Learners Program, expressed her disappointment openly during orientation when she realized that the program was for women. She said, "I have problems with women. All my friends are guys." Margarita said that she "ain't never had a girlfriend." Tashawna told me, "women have a problem with other women." Lucky's comments about her feelings when she first joined the program reveal how protecting herself was a key element of her criticism of others:

> I don't think about the other girls. I worry about myself. Because there's girls here who've been here for two years, and they still haven't went for nothing. You know? I don't think about them. I think about myself getting the work done. . . . They're scared. They have low self-esteem. That's the way I see it. You know? I come here, I don't expect all the teachers to help me. I don't expect all the students to help me. If I feel I need to work on my own, I will. So I don't worry about nobody else that comes to this class.

Among the women, conflicts and negative feelings arose on the basis of attitude, welfare status, and ethnic background. Often these issues intersected. A number of the Project Hope mothers criticized women who "think they are better" than them. A few criticized women whom they believed were participating in the ALP to "keep welfare out of their case." In a writing class one day, Diva, who was not on welfare but received SSI benefits, said that she thought welfare mothers should "get off their asses and try to find a man to support themselves." Her comments infuriated the other women. Jessica, Soledad, Angela, and Yolanda, all Latinas, immediately began talking in Spanish among themselves, saying, "Who does she think she is? Does she think she's better than us? Does she think her shit don't stink?" All the women were talking at the same time, and Diva left the room. Elizabeth tried to explain Diva's outburst by saying, "She's from another culture and just doesn't know." Pam agreed, saying that her boyfriend, the father of her two children, is Jamaican, and "Those Jamaican women think the man should be out there working and supporting them." Ten minutes later, Diva returned to the classroom and the discussion had shifted to the topic of independence. Pam and Yolanda argued that they "don't need a man," and that they could take care of themselves and their children.

Diane, the writing teacher, took this discussion as a learning prompt and encouraged the women to write about their feelings on these issues. Olivia wrote eloquently of the connections between self-esteem and criticizing others:

> I'm tired of just because I live off AFDC [Aid to Families with Dependent Children] people think I am less than everyone else, cause I know I'm not. And the reason why I said this is because I have a friend that is always talking about mothers on AFDC and it gets me mad. She was on it too and now just because she has a job she criticizes everyone else that lives off AFDC. When I pass my GED test and accomplish my goal and find the job I want, I will never criticize no one that is going through the same situation I was in. No one is perfect and we're here for a reason. I wish we could stop criticizing each other and let everyone live their life the way they want to.

In Olivia's words, we can see an awareness—even a critical consciousness—of the value of women supporting each other.

Diane, Robin, and other teachers encouraged the Project Hope women to think critically about the stories of women who had similar life experiences. The Project Hope women began to see how the root causes of violence and their cultural expectations about parenting were tied to social, political, and economic inequities in society. As the women learned more about each other's lives, they began to see how much they had in common. Elizabeth, who graduated in 1998, described this learning experience:

> We talked, we got to know each other, we got to know our background, each other's background. Project Hope made sure that we introduce each other, every new face that came in, we'd introduce, we'd talk a little bit about ourself. We knew that we all was on welfare, and it put more togetherness. Where it was in high school, being in high school, I mean, you had some that learned on a different level, some that wasn't learning, that learned on a lower level, they kind of were pushed out. The teachers mostly focused on the kids that knew the stuff. At Project Hope, rather, we knew that the people that learned on a lower base than others, were no shame or different, 'cause we were all being taught the same thing. And, the teachers, they saw to slow down more for the ones that had to get there. And I like that it was a slower pace, and the ones that didn't understand are still moving to the people that understood it. The teachers mostly focused on the ones at that point who didn't really understand, and kept them, and helped them to get on our level. And the students there were patiently waiting, and they understood, too, because of the friendship and the family and the group thing. They understood and that made it a lot easier for myself, 'cause I know I'm a slow learner.

Elizabeth revealed how the sense of community that developed in the Adult Learners Program in turn became integral to the learning process, supporting the women not just in their lives but in their educations.

Social Inequality

In popular education classes, political cartoons were effective codes for facilitating dialogue, critical reflection, and action. In order to pass the GED social studies test, the women had to learn how to analyze political cartoons. The issues in the GED political cartoons represented the dominant ideology. For example, I examined political cartoons in five different GED "official practice tests" and found that political symbols such as "Uncle Sam," the bald eagle, the Republican elephant, and the Democrat donkey were among the most common images. The majority of the cartoons were related to major events in American history. Teachers in the ALP supplemented the examples from the GED practice tests with contemporary political cartoons from the editorial pages of the *Boston Globe* and *Editorial Humor,* many of which were related to welfare reform, unemployment, and social class. However, the most interesting political cartoons were those developed by the women themselves.

Editorial cartoon by Elizabeth

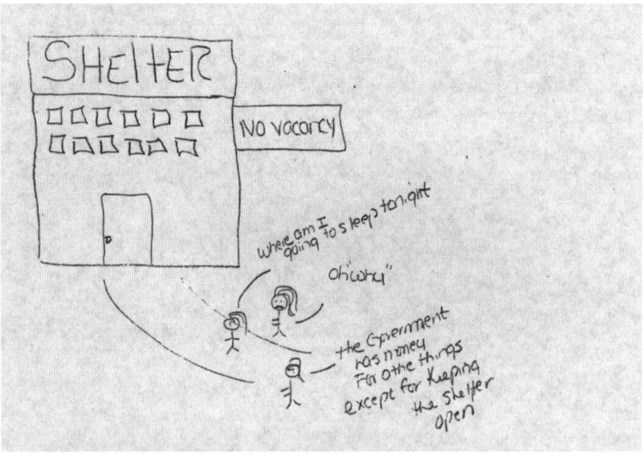

Editorial cartoon by Lucky

Editorial cartoon by Lisa

The women created political cartoons that expressed their opinions about welfare reform and homelessness (see figures No. 6, 7, 8). They also wrote editorials about the need to increase the minimum wage and federal housing subsidies (known as Section 8). These editorials were used as codes in classes and the women sent their letters to their local newspapers. We can see, in the following examples, how the women used their own economic experiences to support policy arguments:

Elizabeth's editorial: I feel that the minimum wage should go up for the simple fact that it's too many women depending on welfare, not because they want to stay on it but because they cannot afford to work. The reason why is because minimum wages is $5.25. How can a single mother support even one child off that? It's being done because of no choice but it is very hard. I have three kids and $5.25 an hour cannot support me and my children, babysitting will run about $2 hundred a week at the least, rent is $650.00 or more, food is $200 for 2 weeks, then light bill, gas bill, etc. In order for a single mother to take care of herself and her children, to keep a roof over their heads, clothes on their back, she needs to make more than $5.25 an hour.

Yvette's editorial: Section 8 has been able to help many people get apartments that can be affordable to them. Section 8 has helped me. Without Section 8 I think more people would be homeless, because they wouldn't be able to afford apartments. Apartments are very expensive. Section 8 relieves people's pockets, even though Section 8 doesn't put you in the exact place you want to be. But it does give you a secure place without worrying when or if you have next month's rent.

The generative themes related to "Social Inequality" ranged from welfare reform to homelessness, to lack of living wages and immigration. In one critical thinking class, the generative theme was immigration, and the code used that day was a poem by Pedro Pietri entitled, *The Broken English Dream.* One stanza in Pietri's poem elicited strong responses from the women:

To the united states we came
To learn how to misspell our name
To lose the definition of pride
To have misfortune on our side
To live where rats and roaches roam
in a house that is definitely not a home
To be trained to turn on television sets
To dream about jobs you will never get
To fill out welfare applications
To graduate from school without an education
To be drafted distorted and destroyed
To work full-time and still be unemployed. (1973, p. 13)

The teacher, Mimi, asked, "What problems do you see in Pietri's poem and have you ever experienced any of them? Why do these problems exist? What can be done to solve them?" The women talked about why immigrants leave their homelands to come to the United States. Helena described her family's immigration to the United States because of widespread poverty in Haiti. Although she could relate to Pietri's poem, she defended the United States, arguing that "there are more opportunities here than in Haiti." Helena also said she missed Haiti, but she would not want to return unless there were significant changes in the government. She said that people here always misspelled and mispronounced her (real) name, and she spoke about her struggles learning English. She also said that people at the nursing home where she worked often "take advantage" of Haitian women by not paying them for overtime. She suggested that more social services were needed to help undocumented immigrants learn about their rights. Helena said, "They have fear, because in Haiti, we live with fear."

Holly really liked the poem. For five years she had lived on the streets in New York City and was a squatter in an abandoned building in the Bronx. She explained how she and her homeless friends would go down into the basements of abandoned buildings and turn on the water and other utilities. Holly said, "[The utility companies] wouldn't know for about six months, and when they found out we were using the water, they would send someone over to shut it off. As soon as that guy left, we'd send our guy back down to turn it up again." She said, "People look down on you, treat you like you ain't worth nothing, all because you ain't got money. I'm smart, I'm not stupid, but I'm poor." Holly connected multiple forms of oppression in society when she said, "Poor people are like immigrants."

The women in this class decided to investigate the types of social services available to recent immigrants and to publicize this information in all of the family shelter's programs. Over a three-week period they collected pamphlets from organizations that help immigrants, and compiled a list of local adult education programs that offered English for Speakers of Other Languages (ESOL) and citizenship classes. This information was displayed on a bulletin board near the entrance of Project Hope, and pamphlets were placed in food pantry bags. We can thus see how a single code, the poem, led all the way from analysis to action.

Resistance to Popular Education

Not all the women embraced the popular education methodology of the ALP. Because they were accustomed to banking methods of teaching, some struggled to understand the popular education process. The focus on generative themes was criticized by some women, especially when they did not see how the problems being discussed were related to the subject material required for the GED. Other women were frustrated by the holistic focus on the women's lives. Yvette complained about how personal problems could impede academic work:

> There was times that we was down here that Georgia's sitting here and Susan's sitting here and I gotta wait for Georgia to finish her telling her what happened to her before we even work on a fraction. There's times that we was upstairs that, Pam, or whatever her name is, is mad and we had to wait for them to calm her down before we get on a problem, you know before we start reading or something. . . . You know, many people come here complaining about what goes on in their house. And then they bring the problem here and then you have to wait for them to feel good before you start working on it. And I don't think it's fair for the teachers because they're ready. . . . But they gotta wait to, you know, talk to the person that's upset or the person that don't wanna read. Now, come on! You're in school. How can you not wanna read when they tell you to read a paragraph that's shorter than, it's a two sentence paragraph and you can't read it?

A number of women would refuse to participate in activities they did not see as relevant to the GED. Some of these activities included workshops with guest speakers about health, housing, and welfare, field trips, arts activities, conferences, neighborhood events, and holiday celebrations. These women were typically older, held full-time jobs before enrolling in adult education classes, and had lived in stable housing for at least five years. (However, there were other women who shared these attributes but actively participated in all aspects of the ALP.) The resistance to participating in such activities was particularly strong from women who were "born-again" Christians. These women did not want to be reminded of their "old selves," sometimes refusing to discuss or write about their past experiences. They believed they were "reborn" and judged other women harshly, even though they had similar backgrounds. They used language such as "those women" to separate themselves from other students, and they were more likely to ask a teacher, "Is that gonna be on the GED?"

These sentiments are captured in the following excerpt from my field notes about a conversation with Rhoda and Rachel, both conservative Christians:

> Today I spoke with Rhoda and Rachel about responsibility and obligation. Our conversation began when I asked Rhoda if she was coming

> to the Holiday Party and she got upset. She said, "Now there you go again, you know I don't go for that kind of thing. I never have and never will." And Rachel who was eavesdropping interrupted and said, "Can I ask you something? Why is it that we are obligated to attend all these things, pot lucks, pizzas, and so on? Why wasn't this discussed during the orientation? Are we mandated to attend these things?" I said no, but that I wondered why she wouldn't want to attend a gathering for fun and relaxation. She took issue with this saying she came to the Adult Learners Program for her GED. She said, "I know what I wanted when I walked in here. The teachers here really care, they are passionate about what they teach. The learning has opened up a world for me and I'm grateful." She talked about how she, "gave up my job caring for children, earning two paychecks a month. Nobody knows I am pursuing my education. Only Claudette and my mother. Nobody knows what I do during the day, where I spend my mornings." She used herself as an example, how she was homeless but didn't let it defeat her. How she comes from a family of "strong" women. She says she "had it in me" . . . "that drive to be better." I asked her how she became that way, but she kept saying she just had it in her. "There's nothing you could do here, but provide the tools for people, who have to pick them up and use them." She was disgusted that people came to class without the right books and without "tablets." She liked that Pat lectures people about not doing their homework, saying that talking to adults like they were children was okay if they acted like children. While she was talking about the women in the group she referred to them as "these people."

Rachel was a proud woman who owned her own business but was secretly hiding her illiteracy. She had internalized hegemonic notions about individual motivation and responsibility and believed that she had a special drive within her that helped her overcome homelessness. Rachel referred to her classmates as "these people" so she could distance herself from them. Yet although Rachel always refused to share personal details about her life, she continued to participate in the program and later facilitated two community meetings to petition the city for a tot-lot so children in the neighborhood would have a safe place to play. Clearly, the ALP's advocacy orientation had affected her.

The few women who held traditional views about school refused to participate in activities that they did not see as directly related to the GED. However, even these women's attitudes changed over time, as they worked together on class projects and developed a sense of community with others. I observed that even the most reluctant women, those who claimed not to care about others, such as Tashawna, Lisa, and Lucky, later assumed mentoring roles in the program. For example, Tashawna had outstanding attendance in the program, and she took on the responsibility of contacting women who were absent to see if they were in trouble. Because several women did not have telephones, Tashawna would visit them when they missed school. Lucky and Pam helped develop a teacher's guide about welfare reform and they coordinated workshops in the community about welfare rights. At first, Lisa rarely spoke in classes, often sitting quietly in a corner, but she later coordinated a peer-tutoring project and developed a computer skills manual for other students. The community focus of the ALP was an indisputably powerful force.

Conclusion

As I have outlined in this chapter, the popular education classes at the ALP used dialogue to foster critical reflection about commonly shared problems and issues. The women in the ALP return to school as adults despite homelessness and other crisis situations because they believe that by "finishing school" and obtaining their high school diploma, they will solve their problems. Without emotional or material support from boyfriends, friends, or family, the women "do what it takes" to provide for their children. The women want their children to have a "better life," and their love and commitment to their children motivates them to participate in adult literacy classes, despite the fact that the odds are against them.

Bee (1993) found that "women who initially enter [critical literacy] classrooms with trepidation and doubts that they belong there gradually discover confidence and power within themselves as they come to understand that the social and political constraints that limit their lives are neither of their own making or immutable" (p. 128). The Project Hope women's relationships strengthened over time as they discussed commonly shared problems in classes and as they worked together on group projects. A group of women described what they "expect" from each other:

> *Tashawna:* I expect their support. You know when I need help, I expect that I can feel comfortable. And I can go and talk to them and ask them for help. Could they help me? And I expect for them not to feel like they know it all and for me to ask somebody else. I expect for them to help me when I ask for their help. That's what I expect.
>
> *Pam:* Same here.
>
> *Lucky:* Me too. I expect support.
>
> *Tashawna:* But some students are not that way.
>
> *Pam:* Yeah, but that's not the way life goes. 'Cause somebody learned it to teach you, so you teach somebody else.

Pam's comment, "Cause somebody learned it to teach you, so you teach somebody else" embodies the collective spirit of popular education. I observed Delila telling a group of new students, "It's very hard to work and accomplish something if you don't work together." Yvette, who complained about how other women aired their problems in classes, later said, "Coming here gives me more strength to see that I'm not out there by myself. It's not just me."

The women's shared experiences went far beyond their hours in the classroom. In the next chapter, I will describe how the women were changed by their participation in popular education classes at Project Hope. I will describe how the women built a community of support within the context of their popular education classes. Specifically, I will argue that the positive "impact" of popular education is evidenced by the women's efforts to help other poor women and children, by their increased self-confidence and sense of community, by their participation in community change projects, and by their increased participation in their children's education and their ability to advocate for their basic legal rights with regard to welfare, housing, health, and education.

5 *Women of Strength*

> I always know that Project Hope is somewhere that I can go back to and say, "I need help, I'm having trouble here or with this," and that I would be welcome, 'cause that's just how I felt when I was there, and I left there feeling that same way. And to today I still feel that I can still get that support, if needed, from Project Hope.
>
> —Elizabeth.

> I couldn't stay away from Project Hope. I couldn't, I had to go back. And today, I still go back. I go back and get me some strength. I go back to get me some strength. I go right back to Project Hope when I'm down and out, when I don't feel good and feel like I ain't going nowhere. If I'm just sitting home, or I'm going crazy, I go to Project Hope to get me some strength. Yes, I do.
>
> —Pam.

In this chapter, I present the stories of women such as Elizabeth and Pam who were changed by their participation in popular education classes at Project Hope. I draw primarily from in-depth interviews, focus groups, and observations of the women's active resistance to changes in welfare policies, as well as their work in the Women's Economic Justice Project, the Women on the Rise workshops, and the development of a video documentary called *Women of Strength,* to show how they applied what they learned in popular education classes by taking action individually and collectively, inside and outside of the classroom community. Project Hope women circulated petitions to extend the two-year Massachusetts welfare time limit, volunteered in voter registration initiatives, wrote letters to state and federal legislators protesting changes in welfare policies, attended lobby days at the statehouse and met with state legislators, spoke at rallies about affordable housing and welfare reform, and worked as educators at information booths at local health fairs and neighborhood festivals. In addition, the majority of the women who graduated with their GEDs entered the human services field, working as counselors and community organizers to help other women such as themselves.

Project Hope's popular education classes encourage women to "act upon the world" (Freire, 1990) in order to change it. This chapter explores the questions: What is the impact of popular education on the lives of low-income women, their families, and communities? How does popular education foster the development of a critical consciousness and a sense of community? I argue that the positive "impact" of popular education is evidenced by the following:

—Women's efforts and growing desires to help other women in the community;
—Women's increased self-confidence and sense of community;
—Women's participation in community change projects, both within and outside of the popular education classes;
—Women's increased participation in their children's education;
—Women's gains in reading, writing, and numeracy skills, and, for some women, the successful attainment of a GED; and
—Women's increased ability to advocate for their basic legal rights with regard to welfare, housing, health, and education.

Women Helping Other Women

Elizabeth: The women thing was great to me. I mean, we have so much in common, we had everything in common. We were women, we had this in common, and we came there not to impress, not to look good, but we came there to learn, and everybody that came through that door was coming to learn. Not to show off for no guy, or look a certain way. And it helped a whole lot with the women thing. And, I feel that women kind of, have more feeling toward another female, you know? I feel if there was guys in that class the learning thing would be totally off, 'cause you probably wanna keep cool for them [laughs]. And you probably would say, "I get it," just to make them think that you really do got it. I like the women thing. I don't think I would have did it without it being all women.

Elizabeth's comment points to the empowering effects of an all-women environment where the women could focus on learning, not be distracted by men, and help each other as women. Many of the homeless and formerly homeless women who participate in the Adult Learners Program have lost their social networks (Edin and Lein, 1997). When the women first enter the program, they claim to have very little, if any, emotional and material "support." However, through their participation in popular education classes, the women begin to forge or strengthen networks of support, both within and outside the classroom. Together they create the support they need to get through the program and address other obstacles in their lives.

The Project Hope women help other women because they have "been there" and can relate to their experiences. Indeed, the majority of the women have had many traumatic life experiences (see chapter 3), and because the popular education classes provide a space for personal reflection, they learn to comfort and help each other. Even women who had not experienced violence or other serious problems were affected by the collective pain and suffering of the other women. For example, Mina told me:

> I found a mixture of women, most of them were younger than me. And coming from the country, living a totally different life, kinda a very quiet life, it was an experience to just be with them. Because it was like being actually put in a group of wild women. You think wild until you get in and you really get to know the people and realize their pain, and how fortunate I was not to have had my life destroyed. I mean, I feel educational-wise, my life was destroyed, but the other things that they had experienced, I hadn't went through. So my heart kinda went out in a lot of ways with that. It was an experience for me to be here with them.

Developing empathy was a crucial step in the community-building process.

One student, Lisa, refused to speak in classes, and teachers were very concerned about her. Even when teachers asked her questions, she shrugged her shoulders and looked down at her lap. Over time, as she continued to participate in group activities, she began to express her feelings and relate more to the other students. When I interviewed her in the fall of 2005, she was a confident, outgoing woman, eager to talk to me about her experiences at Project Hope:

> I feel like I've grown a lot, a lot! I know a lot more now than I did then. I know how to apply for a job, and I know how to go on the Internet, and I'm more open to people, to talk to people. I used to be so shy. . . . I think I'm a little more passionate and more caring for people, instead of, "Oh, I don't care; that's not me, it ain't got nothing to do with me, and I'm just going to be doing me." And I'm willing to listen to people when they have problems, instead of saying, "I don't have time," this,

> that, and the other. You know, I'm willing to help people if they need it. 'Cause I needed help then.

Repeatedly, the women told me that they wanted to help other women because women helped them. A number became advocates for women in their families. Chauntal helped her nephew's girlfriend, who was being battered by Chauntal's nephew, obtain shelter. Chauntal told her:

> "You want to lose your kids?" "No." "What do you want to do?" I said, "Let me tell you something. I understand you love Eddie. Eddie has no education. You don't either. One of yous has to be the bigger person. You have to get that because these children are with you. You have to go back to school and get your education. If you want to be with him and if he's going to change enough, and stop putting his hands on you and take your money that welfare gives you, fine. But he has to do something with his life. Either get a job or go back to school because two dumb parents can't raise no children."

Chauntal clearly had internalized some of Project Hope's most important lessons. Drawing on her own experiences with homelessness and abusive relationships, she advised her nephew's girlfriend to get her education, helped her get into a shelter, and provided emotional support.

Previously, I discussed how a number of women refuse to participate in popular education activities, often asking, "Is that gonna be on the GED?" when classes were focused on generative themes. Chapter 3 highlighted how violence and traumatic experiences in the women's lives made it difficult for them to trust others and thus presented a challenge for the community-building goals of popular education. Yet over time, I observed trusting relationships develop, especially among women who had initially expressed much resistance to working with other women. I observed many instances in which women helped each other inside and outside the classroom. For example, Pam told me: "I asked Lucky for help with my math the other day and she helped me."

The women also see the Project Hope teachers as crucial to their success, as well as to the sense of community in the program. A number of the women described the teachers as "tough" but extremely supportive. For example, Pam was consistently late to class (because her son missed his school bus), and she would often lose her temper with teachers (usually in math classes). Yet years later, Pam appreciatively recalls how Sister Lois pushed and encouraged her:

> I think she was tough because she knew I could do it. She knew it. She seen it in me. Because she said at my graduation that I had a shining light that she always seen. She told me that, and she said, "You have a

> little light inside of you that shines." She said, "And I was hoping that I brought it out, and now you're here, so I know I brought it out." And she was always on my back, because she knew that I could do it. And she knew I needed that push, 'cause a couple times I said, "Sister Lois, keep getting at me, I'm a get it right, I'm a get it right." I just need that help, you know? And sometimes if she didn't talk to me, I used to do little things so she'd yell at me. I'd say, "Oh, you're here, huh?" I'd say, "You're here, Sister Lois!"

Mahogany explained how the teachers fostered a supportive environment: "They made it personal. They didn't come at us like, 'I'm the teacher, I'm the professor. You're the person coming back after twenty years.' They didn't make it seem like we were wasting time. They made it like, it's okay to be coming back twenty years. It's okay to come back twenty years later. You know? You're never too old to learn. . . . But you had to learn everybody's in the group together, we all don't know it, and we're not gonna make everybody feel bad about it."

The sense of community carried over outside the classroom as well. Elizabeth was ready to give up on her GED, but another student would not let her quit:

> One Saturday morning when I was like so stressed and I was so frustrated and I had to go do my last test, to make up the extra points that I needed, and that morning, my friend called from the program, and she was like, "You ready? I'll come pick you up now." I'm like, "I'm not going, I don't wanna go, I can't do this." And she talked to me and she goes, "You know what? I'm coming to get you, and we're gonna go, and we're gonna take our test, we're going, we're going." And I'm like, "I'm not going, I don't want to go." And she kept saying, "Yes, you are." She said, "You only need four more points, that's all you need. Come on, four points!" I said, "I don't wanna go." And she came to my house, and she's like, "Come on." I wasn't dressed. She's like, "C'mon, you got time," she said, "Come on, come on," and we got there, and we had to run 'cause if you get there late, you know? And I was pregnant with my son; she's like, "Come on, come on, come on, let's go!"

Elizabeth took the test and passed, but her friend did not. She said, "I think about her and I really thank her for doing that for me." She explained that this experience embodied the way the women in the program helped one another: "I mean, that's just the closeness, how it was, it was just so close. Everybody wanted to see everybody succeed, you know? No one was really happy if the next person didn't [pass the GED]. And I mean, with me, I sort of feel kind of guilty when I did get more points than the people I went with to do it, but they did it, and you kept on saying, 'You are going to do this, you are going to do this.'"

Women's Sense of Self and Community

The women's participation in popular education classes had an impact on how they perceived themselves. Many of the women did not believe they could complete their GEDs, and their friends and family did not think they would finish either. One woman, who chose the pseudonym "T," described how her sense of self shifted dramatically when she graduated in 1997. Where once she saw herself as a quitter, now she knew she could accomplish whatever she set out to do:

> I'd never finished too much of anything, I would start with something and then I'd stop. I mean, start it and stop it. And I was, like, well, I'm gonna finish it, 'cause I want to get my GED and I want to go on. And my health wasn't doing so good, but I was like, I'm determined. You know? 'Cause I had a child, a couple of them, and I wanted to show 'em no matter how ill you get or whatever, you can still get your education, no matter what. So that's what I did, and I finished, and I actually did it. And I was proud of myself when I showed them, no matter what, you can move on and further your education, no matter what.

For Pam, simply entering the program transformed her life on a daily basis, providing her with the motivation to structure her time so that she could achieve her goals:

> When I made that date, when I made that commitment to this program, I put myself in order 'cause to follow this program you have to have a chart. . . . I just put my whole life on a schedule and now I go according to the schedule. . . . I even got time to do homework because I put homework in there too. I mean, there ain't no more Ricki Lake [a television talk show host] and all that. It's time for the homework. . . . You have to put stuff in order to keep carrying on to be here every day. Because if it's not in order, I ain't gonna get here, you know? So I have my life in order and the things I have to do every day and it's a big jump for me because before I would just do anything any time of the day and it didn't make a difference. Like I did what I wanted to do any time of the day, but now I have plans. I have a time to get up. A time to eat. A time to sleep. A time to cook. Time to do homework. Time to pick up the kids. I have everything in order and every day it fits in. It fits in perfect. I got myself together [laughs]! For real!

Many women also challenged other people's expectations of them. Lucky explained, "It was really a surprise to a lot of people, because as I was growing up running around the street a lot of people didn't think I was going to accomplish anything. So by having that GED, that high school diploma, I'm telling people, 'Hey, I just got my high school diploma when I was thirty years old.' They're like, [whisper] 'Wow, you really went back to school and got it.'" Pam, who graduated in 1998, was clearly proud of herself, but her accomplishments were magnified by the response of her family:

> Oh, they was like, "Mrs. Professor." You know, they had their little names, and stuff. And then I started to talk very intelligent, I start to change a little bit, and I said, "I'm smart now, I got my GED!" My mother was so happy for me, 'cause she said she never had a chance to go back. Oh, my mother got real sentimental with me. And when I graduated, after we went home, she was talking about her. She wishes she could have went back, but they didn't have those types of programs. . . . The family was happy, my kids was like, "*Please,* my mother . . ." They used to go to the school, they would talk about their mother, you know how kids talk about their mother? My daughter be like, "My mother got her education, my mother works at Project Hope." They was so proud that I worked at Project Hope, they were so proud that I was doing stuff with my life. . . . My mother, my father, and my brothers and them, my brother was like, "One more to go now, he need to go back and get his. He need to go back and get his. You got yours."

Project Hope clearly had a ripple effect. As women such as Pam achieved their goals, they inspired those around them. When T got her GED, she told me, "My daughter was like, 'I want to finish school, I like school.'" Anna's uncle, who had pressured her to quit school and get a job, watched her get a high school diploma and decided he wanted to return to school too. "Now, all my family want it now," Anna announced proudly.

Women Becoming Advocates

The women in the ALP supported one another with things such as friendship, child care, and transportation that met their basic material and emotional needs. But the women also helped other women by serving as "advocates" for legal rights related to welfare, housing, health, and education. These advocacy activities, an extension of lessons learned in popular education classes, went beyond the provision of immediate basic needs. Several women I interviewed said that they learned about their rights and how to "stand up for myself" while in the Adult Learners Program. For some, such as Chauntal, just learning how to stick up for themselves and their children was a big step:

> [The Adult Learners Program] was tough, but then it was fun too. . . . There was a lot stuff that, they showed us how we should do, you know? It better involved us, ourself to learn how the system, how the system

> can work for you and how they can work against you. So, that was really good. . . . I stayed involved, there's just a lot of stuff I be fighting now with the Boston Public School system in regards to my children which I think, [the ALP are] the ones that gave me that backbone to don't take no. Because there's hope, you know? That's what I consider I really got from the program is that even with me living here [in Project Hope] how they had me fight for my housing like if welfare told me, "Oh no well, you don't qualify, you can't get this." They showed me well, you can write an appeal because they don't have no reason to refuse you. . . . They push, they push you a lot to say, "No, you *can* do it!"

Others used their new-found advocacy skills on behalf of their communities. Pam, a representative to her housing development, explains how her neighbors were taken advantage of by their housing managers:

> [The management are] scared of me 'cause I don't hold no punches and I be for real. When they sold it, I said, "How you let Boston Housing sell this under you?" I said, "We gonna get these ugly private managements that want to throw us all out." The girl came to me and said, "They're acting, they're acting ugly." I said, "Yeah. I told you all. You all so growner than me, thinking no." I said, "Let me tell you something. All these chicks taking Section 8, the bottom of it say, 'You can't come back.' What is this? You all are not reading the fine print!" They love it when you don't know nothing! I'm not educated bookwise, but I bet you when it comes to surviving, you might not survive, but I will.

Pam's analysis of the situation reveals her understanding of cultural capital and the exercise of power (Bourdieu, 1977). She knows from experience how the poor and uneducated are taken advantage of by those in power.[1] She is an articulate advocate for the power of education and activism. Pam epitomizes the sense of confidence Project Hope helped the women develop, a sense of confidence that is grounded at once in the power of academic achievement and a commitment to community: "As an organizer at Project Hope, I learned from a lot of people. My life has changed—I was in society, people was calling me, looking for me, and they still do. So, it made a big impact on my life. My GED made a big difference in my life. Where now, I'm not afraid to learn. I'm not afraid to take jobs. I'm not afraid to help. I know my place. And my place is helping others. You know? It made a *big* impact on my life."

Many of the women actively participated in Project Hope's advocacy efforts. In follow-up interviews, they talked about enjoying lobbying days to the Massachusetts State House, observing legislative hearings, testifying in front of committees, or participating in rallies and protests. Lisa said that when she was a student at Project Hope her favorite community activities were "When we went to the State House. Because there was a lot of protesting about welfare reform and everybody was really serious about what they wanted to happen. That made a big impact on my life." Such activities gave the women a sense of political empowerment and ownership, as Elizabeth describes:

> I have a lot of memories. I remember going to the State House. We went inside the rooms where they represented, and it was kind of weird because I stood there, and I watched the whole thing. But that night, or a few nights later on, I watched it on TV, and every other time, I would turn my TV from that. I was interested in it because I've been there and I was standing there, right there, at the same spot that was showed on television, it was like, "Wow!" I was able to say, "Oh, I was there!" to the people that were around me. "I was there. I was right there, in that room the other time."

In chapter 2, I discussed how the Project Hope women produced a video documentary called *Women of Strength: Four Stories from the Welfare Debate.* The purpose of the video was to address the misconceptions that were shaping the welfare debate by presenting facts, confronting stereotypes, and "humanizing" the debate with stories of real people. The ALP received a small grant from the Adult Literacy Resource Institute to develop a viewer's guide to accompany the *Women of Strength* video. This project, "Women on the Rise," proposed to train welfare recipients to facilitate critical discussion about welfare reform and become stronger advocates for women on welfare. The video was presented in different settings to a variety of audiences that included college students, business leaders, social service providers, and other community groups throughout the state of Massachusetts.

The welfare reform workshops facilitated by Project Hope women were critically important because "lawlessness" and human rights violations were pervasive in welfare offices between 1996 and 1998 (Withorn, 1999). For example, Angela's caseworker did not want to approve a voucher so she could place her daughter in day care and continue to attend classes at Project Hope. Although Angela was entitled to receive a child care subsidy, she had to quit the program for a couple of weeks while her case went through an appeal process. The *Boston Globe* published an editorial about her case highlighting the punitive measures of the Department of Transitional Assistance and the discriminatory powers of individual caseworkers who determined whether welfare recipients were worthy of receiving assistance. When I spoke to Angela in the fall of 2004, she told me that she still thinks about the *Boston Globe* article and the difference it made: "Welfare helps you on one side, but another side the caseworkers feel like they're giving you money out of their own pockets. She did not want to give me that voucher. I wouldn't have been able to finish school. I mean, if it wasn't for that article, that article really helped. It got everything right, 'cause a lot of people were like, 'um-hm'; it opened their eyes."

Although many of the Project Hope women do not attend or participate in community meetings as much as they would like to, owing to the pressures of work and child care, the majority vote in local and national elections. When I asked Angela if she votes, she said, "Yes. You made me vote! Yes!" Lucky registered voters at the food pantry and reminded everyone in the Project Hope community to vote. T described how she volunteers to register people to vote and convinces them that voting matters, clearly articulating the relationship between voting and power:

> I was out there, getting people to register, and I said, "Now, T, you get people to register, but you ain't voted since I don't know when. You need to get out there and start voting." I was even getting my brother, he got out of jail. Oh yeah, I was getting a lot of them, we was helping people register to vote. And it's amazing how a lot of people wouldn't register. I said, "how can you expect to get a street light fixed, get your street fixed? You're supposed to vote, you know? You see why different places look better than different places? 'Cause they vote, and you all don't, so you need to vote, and you can get the same thing, you know?"

As one of the most active women in her community, T's efforts aim toward helping the young people in her community find a different path:

> I've participated with the Head Start very much. I do fund raising and all that, so, I raise a lot of money for different things. I raised money for when I did the banquet, $2,000—that was for the community, for the children—for my son's Head Start I did a Mother's Day raffle that was $700. And just Valentine's, we just made $423 for Valentine's [Day]. So, I'm pretty much about anything for kids, I'm pretty much there, you know? Because they're our future. So you have to be there and show them. A lot of them is very misguided, and you get to them and talk to them and they'll pretty much be okay. But you think they all hard core and stuff, but pretty much some of them are very smart and they know what they're going to do, what they want to do, and what they want out of life. . . . Some of them have just followed the wrong crowd sometimes. And they need to have some more stuff for these kids, so they won't be out in the street, hanging on the corners and nothing like that. But a lot of these after-school programs and after-school stuff is very expensive, and some of the parents can't afford it. . . . 'Cause I went through a lot

> of stuff, I don't want them to go through it. They don't have to. There's no need for it, so if you can talk to 'em, they can go on and maybe might change their life.

Like the other women at Project Hope, T is determined to transform not just her own life, but the lives of those around her.

Women and their Children

The women in the popular education program overwhelmingly believe that education is important for themselves and their children. Their own struggles in school inspire them to be good role models for their children. The popular education classes increased the women's abilities to advocate for their children and to become more involved with their children's educations. For example, I observed how women offered advice on how to deal with their children's teachers and principals as well as how to find a good kindergarten. Many of the women's children were in special education classes and they worried about their progress and worked hard to support them. Chauntal told me, "I'm fighting the school system to get [my son] into a school that's full day where he's gonna benefit, where he's gonna learn something because he has learning delays."

As noted earlier, the majority of the women return to school for the sake of their children. Delila was not able to help her son with his homework until she gained the literacy skills she needed to understand the material. Her newly acquired skills clearly affect both his attitude and his ability to do his work:

> We sit down and do our homework. They do theirs, I do mine. And, before, he never asked me for help, he look at his homework, if he could not do it, he put it back in his bag, he never asked me for help. Now, when he comes and he looks at his work and he puts aside what he needs help with, and then he does what else he needs to do. And he goes like, "Mummy, mummy, I need your help." "In what?" "In my homework." I say, "How am I supposed to help you?" [teasing him] "I help you! Why don't you help me?" That's what he says!

As the women and their children studied together, education became a common bond for the family. The women and their children learned together and supported one another's educational goals. Numerous studies suggest a strong link between parental involvement and literacy practices in the home and the academic achievements of children (Fingeret and Drennon, 1997; Purcell-Gates, 1995; Ripke and Crosby, 2002; Taylor and

Dorsey-Gaines, 1988; Valdes, 1996). The women especially stressed the importance of reading to their children. Elizabeth fully appreciates the value of setting a good example:

> I'm always constantly on them, and their homework, and the reading, because reading was very important, I learned. And it's true; everything that we learned to read, read, read. 'Cause I was a real slow reader. Then, I was reading, reading, and reading whatever. You know you can always take the newspaper, whatever—just read. . . . Because now I'm able to pronounce things better when I read, and I notice my kids they want to read. They see me reading and that's something that they want to do. Like get their encyclopedia here and they want to read. But if I didn't have that love for reading, I don't think I'd be able to tell them how important reading was.

I heard the women say repeatedly that they wanted their children to have opportunities that were not accessible to them, such as college. Delila said, "I don't really care about my life that much. What I care about is the future of my children. The only thing I say is if I finish school, if I had any support from anyone about school, I wouldn't be here. I want to give my kids that support that I didn't have." The women want to provide a safe environment for their children and they take active steps toward improving their children's circumstances in the face of inhospitable environments. Chauntal knew what her son needed and she set out to get it:

> My son is getting too old, starting to grow up, and there's too much happening around him and I don't want him getting involved. So, I'm the type, I go out there. . . . About three weeks ago I had pulled over a police officer and he was in them vans that pick up the kids—Boston Youth Workers—and I told him, "Look, my son needs to get involved. I don't like where I live at. I don't like what's happening in my neighborhood and he needs to come out of it." So he gave me an application. He says "sign" and he put my son right in.

Other women focus their attention on school. Lucky wants to find a different school for her son:

> It's a terrible school, where he's at, the Dearborn Middle School. You know? You got security, you got weapons, you got kids bringing crack, coke, knives, everything to school. So, that's the peer pressure within his class, all the young thug kids and stuff. He's the only light-skinned kid in his class. So I'm trying to get him into a charter school, where it's more mandatory, like they started with the uniforms and they don't have that type of stuff. It really makes the kids think a whole totally different way. So Junior now is dressing the way he wants and comes home with

> an empty book bag, because the teachers don't give him homework. So I'm trying to change him into a mandatory school that would better educate him and help him stay in line, and really focus more.

Elizabeth successfully obtained scholarships for some of her children to attend private schools, and she is determined to find a way to help the others: "I'm just so happy that I'm able to do this, to try to escape some of the negativity. You can't escape everything, but some. So then I have the two that are in public school, the two middle kids, which are my two youngest daughters. I have one more, next year she'll be in the eighth grade, so she's got one more year in public and then I'm gonna put her in private. I don't know how! But I'm sure God will make a way, and something will come up so I'm able to." For Chauntal, the challenge of trying to meet her children's special needs was itself a learning experience:

> Even though that year that I was out of school, there was a lot of stuff I was learning because my daughters was in special schools. I have [twins], and my two boys have attention deficit disorder so, I was learning about dealing with children with special needs, learning disabilities. Plus, my daughters who was special needs. They got occupational and physical therapy. So, I was learning still. A lot of people is like, "How did you do it? How can you do it?" I had to go speak at the child psychiatry and they wanted to know a lot about how things been going with my son because I've been in domestic situations—I've been battered and stuff like that. They're like, "How can you do it? How can you deal with a four-year-old with an attention deficit disorder, a twelve-year-old with an attention deficit disorder, with a learning disability?" My four-year-old has a behavioral problem, and I'm fighting the school system to get him into a school that's full day where he's gonna benefit, where he's gonna learn something because he has learning delays.

The process of negotiating with both the schools and their children can often be difficult. T is trying to keep the lines of communication open with her daughter's teachers:

> Now, the teachers email me. So I have them email me so we know what we have to do, you know? So that way, when [my daughter] tells me, "No," and she's getting it wrong, I be like, "Here's the email, this is what you're supposed to do." But I tell 'em that they're doing good—now their grades are going down—but I told them, "If you don't start doing better, I'm going to have them keep you back, 'til you get it right." I said, "I understand." . . . So we're having a conference this week at the end, with the teacher. 'Cause my daughter she was doing real good in her child school. Now she goes to high school, she's not doing so good. There's a big difference.

Still, T is often frustrated that teachers only call her when there are behavioral problems: "Why, if they have got a academic problem, you're supposed to speak on it, but if it's a behavioral problem, oh, you'll call right away. You know, what is wrong with this picture? I don't get it. You know what I mean? So, they need help. If it's behavior, then I understand it, because that's like harming another student or something, or harming themselves. Okay. But what about the academic? They're not getting that, they need help with that also."

But though many of the women struggle with their children and the schools, Yvette sees the results of her efforts in her children's goals, and she is determined to help them achieve those goals:

> So that's the kind of pressure I put on my daughters. I always tell 'em, "I'm doing this not for you to flunk school. I'm doing this for you. You know what I'm saying? I want you to be somebody." And right now, my youngest daughter, she wanna work at the fire department and she wants to be a nurse. [laughter] And then Aida, she wants to be a cop and she wants to be a lawyer. So they have expectations. They know what they wanna be. I'm just there to make sure that they follow up on it.

Women's Goals for the Future

When the women first enroll in the ALP, during a student orientation they are asked to share their goals for the next five years. At first, this exercise is very difficult for them. Many say, "I just want to get my GED, then I'll think about work." As the women make gains with regard to their literacy skills, a counselor, who is formerly homeless and a graduate of the ALP, helps them develop a career plan. Some women want to go to college and work in business. Others express interest in building trades/construction work or law enforcement. Yvette wants to study electronics:

> All my life I wanted to work with fixing things. Because all my uncles and half my family worked with electronics. Like my cousin, he fixes TVs and he fixes telephones. He will fix your camera. He will fix anything. I mean, he has this electronic equipment that he brought from his job that used to make bird sounds. He know how to make bird sounds. He know how to make elephant sounds. I mean, he had all these things and that's what really interested me 'cause at the time I was fifteen. And then when he started showing me, it wasn't that easy. I thought it was easy but it wasn't that easy. So that's when I really knew that electronics was gonna be a competition. I was like, this is gonna be what I wanna do because this is gonna make me study for what I wanna do. I wanna come by one

> day and say, "Oh yeah, well I'm here to fix a computer that broke down." And just open a computer up and know what I'm gonna do.

However, the kinds of jobs or careers the majority of the women desire are traditional women's work: secretaries, social work, nursing, and other "carework" or helping professions. T, for instance, wants to be a counselor:

> I'd like to be a counselor. Oh, I love counseling. I love helping people, any chance I get. They always come to me for advice, and I sit there talking and listening to them, tell them what they need to do. And if they're not doing good, if people ain't treating you right, then you need to leave them alone, you know? I mean, there's this one guy, a friend of my husband's, he going backwards, and I just don't understand it. He's an older guy, but he's in the same situation: he just went to jail, the girl put him in jail. But why are you still there? You went back there, we're trying to help you find different places and shelters for you to go to, 'cause until you get your own, you're going back there, she's gonna steal your money again. I'm trying to figure how to help him out. Trying to find some connections for him to get into now.

Delila's desire to help people is more explicitly political: "I don't like working with the government because I would be working against the government. . . . See, I like to work to change things, to make better things. I don't care about the money. I don't know why. I never really cared for money. . . . If I'm gonna be a social worker, I want to work with kids. When I say kids, not kids who are born here, but kids who came from another country. Who are very confused."

Delila embodies the goals of Project Hope. Popular education provided the women with the opportunity to critically reflect on their "being in the world" and to actively change it. This desire for change was a common bond in the community of women. Chauntal describes how "the system" of foster care and poverty in which she "grew up" needs to be changed:

> Well, I've been on drugs. I came off the drugs, even though I didn't go through a program because I was scared I would lose my child. I still conquered that. I went to being battered, even though I had the district attorney, nobody could help me. I had to leave Boston and then come back to Boston once he wasn't looking for me anymore, you know? I conquered being battered, learning—knowing I had to leave the situation and keep me and my child out of harm's way and keep anybody from taking my kids. So, it's like, I covered so much. I covered living in a foster home. I feel that Department of Social Services does not stay in touch with children and foster care enough. It should be more. Even if they had to

> send someone else to the home, like people that's coming to internship and have them be doing follow-up on them foster kids, you know what I mean? It's just there's so much stuff about the system that needs to be changed. And because I'm the type of child that grew up in that system, I haven't seen it improve any. I've seen it just get worse.

Chauntal shows a "critical consciousness" as she reflects on her life struggles and understands how these problems continue to impact women such as her (Freire, 1973; 1990). She has not yet achieved all her goals, but this understanding is helping her on her way.

Conclusion

This chapter examined the impact of popular education on the lives of the Project Hope women, their families, and their communities. The National Center for the Study of Adult Learning and Literacy (NCSALL) commissioned a major "study of studies" about the effectiveness and impact of adult education on people's lives.[2] The study focused on both outcomes for learners and "impacts," or "the changes that occur in the family and society at large. . . . Commonly studied variables include individual gains in employment, job quality, and income; reduction of welfare; learning gains in reading, writing, and mathematics; GED acquisition; and changes in self-confidence; . . . the effects on children's reading readiness, participation in children's school activities, and whether learners vote" (Beder, 1998, p. 3). The findings of the twenty-three studies examined by NCSALL researchers were contradictory. Researchers had difficulty determining whether adult basic education had an impact on learners' gains in basic skills because there were differences between objective measures and subjective "self-reports." Beder (1998) suggests that "it could be that self-reported perceptions of the basic skills gain are inflated by the normal human tendency to answer socially acceptable responses and a reluctance to say unfavorable things in a program evaluation. . . . Then again, perhaps the self-report data are accurate and learners are recognizing important gains in themselves that are too small to be measured by tests" (p. 7).

In my research, I found that the women learners do recognize important gains and changes in their lives as a result of participating in adult education classes. No ethnographic studies about the impact of adult education on learners' lives were included in NCSALL's research. Intensive participant observation and interviews with low-income women at Project Hope allowed me to see changes in the women's attitudes and behaviors over time. Throughout this chapter, the women themselves offer strong evidence of popular education's positive impact on their lives. Their participation in popular education classes motivated the women at Project Hope to help other low-income women and children in the community, increased their self-confidence and sense of community, strengthened their involvement in their children's education, and made them feel as if they can make a difference in their communities.

In the next chapter, I explore what happened to the Project Hope women after welfare reform. I argue that the goals of popular education programs that produced the positive results described in this chapter have been subsumed by the drive to help women on welfare obtain the GED credential as soon as possible. Yet research suggests that the GED itself is not sufficient to help these women improve their circumstances. Finally, I present recommendations aimed at addressing the root causes of poverty that truly shape these women's lives.

" We are being denied a basic Education and Productive lives!'

Bring your children to the rally!!

Call for Information at

ZEE-AT (617)442-3355

Brian (671)432-3207

Susan (508)435-1563

6 *Learning to Labor, Laboring to Learn*

> I keep stressing to [my daughter] how important education is. And I tell her that she's my mirror. She has to do things, she has to do this for me, because I was never able to go ahead and finish high school, and go ahead and into college. . . . I just keep telling them that, "You want your high school diploma. You want this. Look at me. All these years, you saw me struggling going back to get this GED, and I struggled and I struggled. Then even after the GED I was able to put myself through trade school, and this is something that I should have been doing a long time ago. But, you see how society, how tough it is, this world is. And, you saw me doing it, getting up, and doing it."
>
> —Elizabeth

When I first met Elizabeth in 1996, I was impressed by her intense focus on passing her GED tests. She was one of the few students who came to class early and stayed late so she could practice taking the "official GED practice" tests that were available to all ALP students. Her teachers told me they were worried about Elizabeth because she was taking the tests every month. Instead of improving her scores, however, Elizabeth sometimes actually scored lower on tests she had already passed, so she became depressed, feeling as if she was back to square one. Her teachers advised Elizabeth not to take the tests so often because they were expensive, and taking them so many times was not effective practice. Instead, they argued, she should work on strengthening her math and science skills, and concentrate on learning new material. But

Elizabeth persisted, continuing to retake the GED tests, over and over, until she finally passed in 1997.

It is easy and inspiring to ascribe a happy ending to Elizabeth's story: she passed the GED, she went to trade school, she is encouraging her daughter to follow her lead. But if we look more broadly at what happened to the women in the Adult Learners Program, a different picture emerges. After welfare reform, many of the women, such as Elizabeth, became increasingly focused on the GEDs, rather than the broader educational aims of the ALP. But between 1995 and 1998, during the height of welfare reform in Massachusetts, 62 percent of the women dropped out of the ALP before completing their GEDs. Of the thirty-one women who dropped out, eighteen left the ALP because of pressures from welfare caseworkers to find employment as soon as possible (they were told "any job is a good job"). Another thirteen women dropped out owing to health problems, or because they moved and did not have reliable transportation to Project Hope.

Because I worked and volunteered at Project Hope over the past decade, I tried to maintain contact with as many of the fifty women as possible. From 2003 to 2005, I was awarded a National Academy of Education Spencer Postdoctoral Fellowship to conduct follow-up interviews with fifteen women; I collected data on an additional ten women (see appendix). Of the twenty-five women I followed up, fifteen completed their GEDs. Four women who had dropped out of the ALP went on to earn their External Diplomas through the Boston Public Schools. Another six women were still studying for their GEDs: Jessica and Lisa told me they were studying on the weekends, and had taken the GED in the past two years (both have severe math anxiety); Diva, Jessie, and Renata had returned to the ALP years later, and were still pursuing their GEDs; Soledad was being tutored by one of the former ALP teachers who was working at another ABE program.

Of these twenty-five women, only Rhoda graduated from college with a bachelor's degree. Helena and Elsie earned their associate's degrees at local community colleges, and, as of 2005, Elsie was enrolled at a local university pursuing her bachelor's degree. Elizabeth, Angela, and Jessica successfully completed medical or office skills training programs at proprietary schools. Fourteen of the women were working full-time jobs (mostly in medical, service, and retail industries) and six were working part-time. Three women were unemployed because of physical disabilities, and two women were at home caring for newborn children. However, each of the fourteen women working full-time jobs said they were not earning enough to support their families, and only three of them had health insurance provided by their employers. The rest of the women were enrolled in the Mass Health program. The women's housing also remained unstable: fourteen women were living in public housing and/or received Section 8 subsidies; eight were living in apartments they shared with extended family; only three women were paying market-rate rent for their housing.

This final chapter asks how we can account for what happened to these women, and what we can do about it. It begins with an exploration of the reality—not the hype—of life for the poor after welfare reform: I present findings from a decade of research about welfare-to-work programs that show these programs alone do not help welfare recipients move out of poverty. Drawing upon interviews with policymakers, researchers, and adult literacy teachers and practitioners, I examine the impact of welfare reform on the ALP, women's literacy, and the adult literacy field overall. Finally, I offer recommendations for an alternative approach to supporting low-income mothers and addressing the root causes of poverty.

The Post-Welfare Reality

Welfare reform has been called a success because of the decrease in the number of people receiving welfare. In Massachusetts the number of families receiving welfare declined from 79,000 to 42,700 families between 1996 and 2001 (Wen, 2007). However, since 2001, the welfare rolls are increasing in Massachusetts, as well as nationally (Parrott and Sherman, 2006). There is strong evidence that the "roaring economy" of the 1990s contributed to the numbers of women on welfare moving into jobs, as much as, if not more than, any laws or policies. Then there are the women who seem to have fallen through the cracks. According to the Center on Budget and Policy Priorities report, *TANF at 10:* "Between fiscal year 1996 and 2004, the number of single mothers receiving TANF fell by two million, yet employment among single mothers rose by only about one million. This left a growing third group—jobless single mothers that receive no help from TANF, or other government assistance programs as well" (Parrott and Sherman, 2006, p. 4).

Regardless of whether they remained on welfare or got jobs, poor women, such as the women of the ALP, continue to struggle. Health problems, lack of transportation, lack of quality child care, depression, and domestic violence continued to be barriers to employment and further education. This is confirmed in Hamilton's (2002) research that found that five years after leaving welfare, 25 percent of former welfare recipients lack health insurance and "a substantial minority of welfare recipients report having recently experienced domestic abuse" (p. 6). According to Moffitt (2002), "incomes of women leaving welfare are only slightly above what they were when the women were on welfare . . . there is a significant group of very disadvantaged women, many no longer on welfare, who have major difficulties with employment because of poor job skills, poor physical and mental health and other problems" (p. 1). The incomes of former welfare recipients remain low because their jobs are often part-time, they are being sanctioned at higher rates, and many states "reduce TANF benefits dollar-for-dollar when earnings increase (at least if women stay on welfare rolls), thereby canceling out any gain in income that might result in increased work" (p. 4). This seems to be the most counterproductive aspect of legislation that is supposed to reduce poverty. In contrast, Parrott's and Sherman's (2006) research shows that increasing "earnings disregards" and expanding "make-work-pay" policies can improve employment outcomes (pp. 8–9).

Research by the National Institute for Literacy has shown that welfare-to-work programs helped people find jobs but did not "give them a leg up to better paying jobs" (D'Amico, 1998, p. 11). Researchers at the Milken Institute, RAND, and the Urban Institute examined the employment prospects of welfare recipients in the most populous U.S. counties (Levenson, Reardon, and Schmidt, 1998). Their findings reveal that "typical TANF[1] recipients have extremely low basic skills. Because of their low basic skills, the vast majority of jobs are not open to TANF mothers. The nation's economy would need to create many more low-skilled jobs to fully employ all welfare mothers. Moreover, even if TANF mothers find employment, many of them will not find jobs that pay enough to lift them and their children out of poverty" (Levenson, Reardon, and Schmidt, 1998, p. 1). Carnevale and Desrochers (1999) also studied the employment prospects of welfare recipients with very low literacy levels who were working in unstable jobs. They found that: "Even when welfare recipients find a job, they often lose it before establishing a period of tenure. Data from several employment and training programs suggest that about 60 percent of recipients lose their first job and that one-third to one-half of all terminations are the result of former recipients either being laid off or fired" (p. 18).

Welfare reform studies also show that many low-income women do not know how to apply for the Earned Income Tax Credit (EITC); in addition, many are not eligible because they have unstable work histories and/or they do not earn enough to qualify for the EITC (Moffitt, 2002).

According to Moffitt (2002), "studies also show welfare leavers experienced declines in their receipt of food stamps and Medicaid," and fewer women are applying for welfare benefits in general (p. 4). These studies only track women for whom there is information: nationally, 25 to 40 percent of women who left welfare are not in the workforce, and little is known about what happened to the welfare recipients who were dropped from the rolls and are not working (Hays, 2003).

Conditions have also been difficult for women who remain on welfare. According to Hays (2003), "Sanctions are the central forms of punishing welfare mothers for their failure to comply with welfare rules—their failure, in other words to behave properly. To be sanctioned means that all or part of your welfare benefits are cut . . . it is estimated that about one-quarter of welfare recipients are under sanction for their failure to comply with welfare regulations—more than double the number of recipients who suffered such punishment prior to welfare reform" (p. 41). Welfare recipients can be sanctioned for missing a meeting with a caseworker, missing GED classes, being late to their workfare jobs, or even getting fired from a job (also see Parrott and Sherman, 2006).

Moffitt (2002) also studied women who left welfare because they reached their time limits or were "sanctioned." He finds that many states granted waivers for the five-year federal time limit for their most disadvantaged families, so it was not until the late fall of 2001 that many families on welfare reached their time limit for receiving public assistance. Moffitt writes:

> More is known about sanctions because they have been in force for most of the time since 1996 and in some cases even before then. Many more women have been sanctioned than have been hit by time limits. The studies of women who have left welfare show that such women are less likely to have jobs than other welfare leavers. This appears to be because sanctioned welfare recipients tend to be less educated, have lower jobs skills, and are in poorer health than other welfare recipients. (p. 3)

T's comments on the tenuous status of welfare recipients support Moffitt's analysis:

> You got to follow up on things. You got to make sure that you have all your papers there. And make sure that they have received your papers. Because they could tell you they don't have your papers, and you waiting and you're wondering why you're not on, or you didn't get no assistance. And sometimes they say they never received. The social worker said they sent them the paper. Sometimes you don't receive it. 'Cause there've been some papers I ain't received. I didn't know there was a paper, why

> you telling me this? And they say they sent it. I'm like, "I thought you sent it. But I haven't received anything." So there's a lot of things like that, that've been going on, that I have seen.

Critics of social welfare programs are quick to assert that "any job is a good job," but this is contradicted by findings from numerous studies, many of them funded by the U.S. government. For example, a national evaluation study, "Moving People from Welfare to Work: Lessons from the National Evaluation of Welfare-to-Work Strategies"[2] (Hamilton, 2002)—considered the most comprehensive study of welfare-to-work programs to date, conducted by Manpower Demonstration Research Corporation (MDRC), and funded by the U.S. Department of Health and Human Services and the U.S. Department of Education—studied the impact of different "pre-employment" approaches to helping welfare recipients move into work. It included programs that emphasized "short-term job search assistance," programs that emphasized "longer-term skill-building activities (primarily basic education) before entering the labor market," and programs that "mixed elements" of these approaches (Hamilton, 2002, p. 1).[3] The report describes the ideology for "work-first" welfare reform mandates:

> Participation mandates in welfare-to-work programs are intended to change welfare recipients' perceptions and behavior in several ways. First, they send the message that receipt of welfare is not an unconditional entitlement. Second, owing to the time investment required by program activities, they reduce the perceived value of welfare grants relative to that of employment. Third, they compel some people who would otherwise not do so to participate in activities that program operators believe will enhance their employability. (p. 20)

This statement suggests that the strategies employed under TANF to reduce poverty rest upon changing individuals' perceptions and behaviors and motivating them to value work. As I described earlier, all of the Project Hope women have worked and value working, yet they are still very poor. Moving welfare recipients into low-paying jobs does not move them out of poverty. Clearly these strategies fail to address the causes of poverty.

I would argue, however, that welfare reform was never intended to really help people move out of poverty. Rather, the point of welfare reform is to terminate "dependent" poor people from the system. Receiving welfare itself is such a dehumanizing experience that it discourages people from seeking help. Sally Tomlinson, in her book *Education in a*

Post-welfare Society (2001), suggests that in a post-welfare society, the poor are irrelevant consumers:

> By the 1990s it had become clear that the poor in developed societies were no longer a reserve army of labour, as earlier analyses described it. Modern societies . . . do not need massive labour forces, profits can be increased while cutting down on labour, and grooming the poor to be a reserve army of labour no longer makes sense. The tragedy for the poor was that modern society engages its members mainly as consumers, and those lacking sufficient income, credit cards, and bank accounts were flawed consumers. Decent and normal members of society, the consumers, want nothing from them and expect nothing. The poor are totally useless . . . for them zero tolerance. (p. 163; see also Bauman, 1998)

Tomlinson (2001) examines the changing purposes of public education in a post-welfare society:

> Governments around the world, who were turning their welfare states into post-welfare societies, were rediscovering human capital theory, with individuals told to invest in themselves in a lifelong process of learning and re-skilling in order to retain any kind of job. . . . Schools, teachers and local education authorities were increasingly held responsible not only for failing individuals, but also for failing to make the national economy competitive in global markets. The roles and responsibilities of local education authorities (LEAs) were increasingly diminished, and the role of private contractors and business entrepreneurs expanded. A language and practice of managerially, of accountability, inspection, testing and targets, precluded debates about the purposes of education beyond preparation for the economy. (p. 2)

In this business-oriented framework, there is, ironically, little room for the individual whose agency neoliberalism purportedly touts. Ten years after welfare reform, neoliberal "market-driven" ideologies continue to shape public policies toward women on welfare, public schooling, and social services for the poor in the United States. Though Tomlinson's work focuses on the contradictions and failures of introducing "market" private-interest reforms in public schools in the U.K., there are remarkable parallels to neoliberal policies and practices with regard to U.S. school reform and the social welfare system in the United States. But, as this chapter shows, the introduction of market reforms in welfare-to-work programs, as well as in efforts to reform public schools, have failed to improve life chances for low-income families. The neoliberal discourses of accountability and responsibility end up stigmatizing poor women and people of color. As I discussed in chapter 1, "Framing the

Blame and Gain," welfare reform policies such as "Learnfare" are intended to police poor families; they punish low-income mothers by cutting their cash assistance if their children are excessively absent from school. Apple (2004) argues that "The fear of the 'racial other' has played a significant role in this discursive construction of the 'problem with the public school'" (p. 72). He writes, "Less funding will be given to public (state supported) schools. A politics of blame will evolve in which parents who have no choice but to keep their children in under funded and highly policed inner-city schools will be seen as the source of the problem of the common school" (p. 78).

We can see the continued dehumanizing effects of both welfare and welfare reform in the persistence of the stigmas of being on welfare that remain deeply embedded in our culture. In Massachusetts the "Full Employment Program" gives employers who hire welfare recipients a $2.50 an hour wage subsidy, and a maximum $1,200 annual tax credit for employing welfare recipients (thus cuts in public assistance to women on welfare shifted to public assistance for corporations). Yet, according to a recent article in the *Boston Globe,* "Job Program for Welfare Recipients Falls Flat" (January 15, 2007), business participation in the Full Employment Program "has fallen dramatically from its peak of 500 employers in 1998 to only 32 businesses today, and the state has stopped enrolling new companies" (Wen, 2007). The program is not appealing to employers because they feel there are too many "risks" for hiring welfare recipients, including "high turnover and greater need for job training," the program is not "cost-effective," and the welfare mothers "weren't committed to stay." State officials acknowledge that welfare recipients often do not want to "reveal that they are on welfare, fearing it might discourage employers from hiring them. That makes it harder for firms to identify applicants who would make the companies eligible for tax credits" (Wen, 2007).

Because of Massachusetts's failing employer incentive programs, the Massachusetts Department of Transitional Assistance is considering new approaches to make sure "welfare recipients do not feel stigmatized." A *Boston Globe* article, "Job Applicants Face Query on Welfare" (December 17, 2006), reveals that many welfare recipients do not want to disclose that they have received welfare benefits when they apply for jobs. Companies such as Best Buy, The Gap, and CVS, in addition to subjecting low-wage workers to personality tests and drug testing, now ask potential job applicants if they have ever received welfare benefits so they can receive tax breaks for these "hard to employ groups" (Wen, 2006). According to the article, "Lawyers and advocates for the poor say these questions reflect a corporate culture insensitive to stigmas endured by those who have been on public assistance" (Wen, 2006). Although employers insist that the questions asked of former and current welfare recipients are voluntary and that their answers do not affect whether the applicant will be hired, it is hard to imagine this is true.

Not only do the stigmas against welfare recipients persist, but so does their criminalization. For example, the Ninth U.S. Circuit Court of Appeals ruled on September 19, 2006, that San Diego County's "Project 100" program could search the homes of welfare recipients without a warrant. The ruling states that using "peace officers" to search the homes of welfare recipients violates neither constitutional rights against unreasonable searches nor privacy rights. According to Judge A. Wallace Tashima, the searches "serve the important governmental interests of verifying an applicant's eligibility for welfare benefits and preventing fraud." They were deemed constitutional because the court argued they are not for "criminal investigation," they take place during normal business hours (unlike the "midnight raids" of the 1970s–80s), and they can only be conducted with the consent of the welfare recipient. The ruling does not recognize that consent is not freely given because benefits would otherwise be terminated. If police were to find an able-bodied adult living in the household who is not "on-record," would the welfare recipient be sent to jail for fraud? This ruling shows the continuing disrespect and distrust society has toward the poor.

McCorkel (2004) suggests there are "parallels" between punitive welfare reform and criminal justice policies and the increase in the population of women in prison. Since 1985, the population of women in U.S. prisons has more than tripled (Tuhus-Dubrow, 2004). A disproportionate number of these prisoners are women of color; black women are three times more likely than white women to be incarcerated. According to Tuhus-Dubrow (2004), "from 1977 to 2003, New York State's female prison population increased by approximately 500 percent—about twice the rate of males—overwhelmingly as a result of the 'war on drugs'" (p. 1).

The United States has the highest reported rate of incarceration in the world. According to Nolan and Anyon (2004), between 1980 and 2000 the U.S. incarceration rate increased 258 percent, and two-thirds of the prison population is racial/ethnic minorities. Though African Americans comprise 13 percent of the American population, they make up an alarming 66 percent of the total prison population: "An astounding one out of every three young Black men are either incarcerated or otherwise involved in the criminal justice system, and for the first time in decades, there are more Black men headed to prison than to college" (pp. 134–35).

According to many researchers, these dramatic increases in prison population owe to Drug War policies such as mandatory minimum sentencing, limits to plea bargaining in the 1980s, and "three-strikes laws" in the 1990s. But education is also clearly implicated: according to ProLiteracy (2006), "research shows that 67 percent of prison inmates are high school dropouts and 70 percent of the more than one million inmates in state and federal prisons are functionally illiterate or read below the eighth grade level" (p. 12).

In the book *Learning to Labor in New Times,* Nolan and Anyon (2004) studied the connections between the prison system and public schools in poor urban neighborhoods. They write: "This school/prison continuum has developed through the use of academic policies such as high-stakes testing, disciplinary policies such as 'zero tolerance,' the use of high-tech security apparatus and police officers in schools, and the establishment of a multitude of intermediary institutions that house youth as they move between educational and custodial facilities" (p. 134). Though none of this research addresses welfare reform, the interconnections between education, incarceration, and poverty are clearly complex and powerful.

Educating the Undereducated in the Post-Welfare Era

The Project Hope women believe they will solve their problems and achieve a "better life" for their children by completing their GEDs. As Sylvia put it, "GED is power to us, and with this power all of our goals will be accomplished." Unfortunately, research studies about the economic power of the GED show mixed results. One of the nation's leading researchers on the GED, Brown University's John Tyler, writes, "Dropouts with very low skills tend to benefit from the GED credential. A GED provides no additional economic benefit, however, to dropouts with higher skills." This is confirmed by Barton (2005): "Earnings of GED holders are less than their counterparts who receive regular diplomas—but more than those without either" (p. 31; Chaplin, 1999). Why is there such a discrepancy? According to education historian Dorn (2003): "Diplomas have an exchange value, either in a labor market or to gain entry to another school, and that exchange value may not be directly related to the purpose of a degree requirement" (p. 19). He suggests we need to consider the "property interest" in a diploma versus the "purpose of the degree requirement" (p. 19).

Dorn examines the dramatic growth of alternative diploma credentials since the 1970s. His research (and others that he cites) finds there are racial differences in terms of who earns alternative diplomas: "Of those who earn some high school credential, white students are more likely than the general population to earn high school diplomas, while Latino/a and African American students are more likely to have alternative credentials" (p. 7). Dorn suggests that alternative credentials may provide a "safety valve for high schools enabling them to slough off responsibility for poor students" (p. 7).

These discrepancies have become even more notable in the last ten years, under the simultaneous influence of welfare reform and education reform. Several policy developments signal a profound change in the nature of the GED in today's educational culture. In January 2001, the Massachusetts commissioner of education and the GED office of Massachusetts changed the GED testing requirements so that test-takers would be allowed only one year to complete the five-test battery (Mechum, 2004). This policy was revised on January 1, 2005, and currently, GED students must still complete the five GED tests within one year, but those who do not pass are allowed two more years (Massachusetts Department of Education, 2006).

Meanwhile, in 2001, the Massachusetts Comprehensive Assessment System (MCAS) "high-stakes" standardized test became a graduation requirement for tenth graders attending Massachusetts's public high schools. According to Balliro (2004), many Massachusetts adult educators were concerned that the MCAS would lead to an increase in dropouts, who would then enroll in ABE classes seeking diplomas. Balliro interviewed Ruth Derfler of the Massachusetts Department of Education, who disputed this, claiming there are many reasons young people drop out, which "predate the test requirement" (p. 15). In a *Boston Globe* article, "Tests Seen Increasing Dropouts" (August 14, 2003), the Massachusetts Department of Education commissioner, David Driscoll, similarly suggested that it was too early to determine the impact of the MCAS on dropout rates, especially given that the dropout rate has remained steady so far. According to Driscoll, "We're really in our infant stage, and I think we need to watch it over years." However, Bob Schaeffer of FairTest, a Massachusetts advocacy organization that is opposed to the MCAS graduation requirement, argues that failing the MCAS could be a "tipping point" in the decision to drop out (Kurtz, 2003). He criticizes the way Massachusetts calculates its passing rates because "students who dropped out between freshman year and senior year or those who have been held back" are not accounted for (Kurtz, 2003, p. 2).

Despite the caveats from the Massachusetts Department of Education, an important shift in dropout patterns has occurred in the United

States. According to Barton (2005), over the past three decades, much of the dropping out of school took place between grades 11 and 12; in recent years, it has occurred between grades 9 and 10. Barton argues that "This is a significant shift, making dropouts younger and less educated than in the past, and therefore facing more difficulty in getting jobs" (p. 13). Though Massachusetts Department of Education officials claim there is no evidence that younger students are enrolling in ABE programs, in discussions with Massachusetts adult educators, they tell me that they have younger students in their GED classes than in the past. This is certainly the case at Project Hope, where younger women have been enrolling in the Adult Learners Program. Nationally, there is evidence that high-stakes testing is pushing younger students into ABE programs. A number of researchers argue that disadvantaged students are being "pushed out": forced into GED programs so that school districts do not get failing grades in meeting the performance standards mandated by the No Child Left Behind Act (NCLB). For example, an Urban Institute study finds there is:

> Pretty strong evidence that the GED option has been encouraging kids to drop out of high schools nationwide. The rules governing the GED have become lenient over time. . . . Under No Child Left Behind, we're holding schools very strictly accountable for test scores, but barely holding them accountable for students who drop out or go into GED programs. It is like holding hospitals accountable for the condition of their patients who leave, but ignoring the number who die. It's a perverse incentive system. (quoted in Arenson, 2004, p. 2)

In addition, Chaplin (1999) and Barton (2005) find the GED increasingly available to and targeted at teenagers because many states have changed their eligibility policies. Now, in many states, sixteen-year-olds can take the GED. Nationally in 1990, 35.8 percent of certificates were awarded to sixteen- to nineteen-year-olds; this percentage rose to 44.6 percent in 2000. Numerically this was a 42 percent increase, from 175,000 to 223,000 (Barton, 2005, p. 31). In Massachusetts, between 1990 and 2000, there was a 19 percent increase in the percentage of GED recipients who were sixteen or seventeen years of age (Barton, 2005 p. 32). Barton writes, "high schools, likely feeling the pressure of the test-based accountability movement and the increased use of exit exams, have diverted students to programs that prepare for the GED" (p. 33).

A recent *Time* magazine article is headlined, "Does a GED Really do the Job: Researchers fear that America's favorite second-chance exam may be exacerbating the dropout problem" (Thornburgh, 2006). The article claims that the "largest high school in America . . . by the sheer number of credentials granted" is the American Council on Education's GED Testing Service, which awarded 400,000 GED certificates in 2004 (p. 1). The article suggests that the GED "functions too often as a siren call for restless teenagers, attractive enough to lure them out of high school, but not so alluring that they actually end up taking it and go on to college. Once a test designed solely for adults, the GED is increasingly becoming a teenager's test" (p. 1).

Haney et al. (2004; cited in Barton, 2005) studied changes in high school enrollment and dropout patterns. The researchers found that, nationally, there has been what they refer to as a "bulge" in ninth-grade enrollments, that is, a trend of increasing enrollments in grade 9. They found that in 2000 there were 440,000 more students enrolled in grade 9 than in grade 8, and attrition between grades 9 and 10 increased. According to the researchers this means that more students flunked and were held back and forced to repeat grade 9 (p. 13). In Massachusetts, this is a particularly significant trend because the tenth-grade MCAS scores are linked to graduation. Public schools in Massachusetts may be holding back more students in the ninth grade to prevent high failure rates. It seems there is fear of punishment from federal school authorities if failing school districts cannot meet the NCLB standards.

Barton (2005) finds that since the 1970s, high school completion rates have been declining across the United States. For example, from 1990 to 2000, the high school completion rate declined in all but seven states (pp. 3–5). At the same time, since the late 1970s, "second-chance" education and training programs (especially ABE) have also seen major reductions in federal and state funding. The National Coalition for Youth Employment estimates that the federal investment in "second chance" education and training opportunities decreased from $15 billion in 1979 to less than $3 million in 2003 (pp. 29–39).

Overall, these statistics point to a growing squeeze on both students and ABE programs. Pushed out of high school, disadvantaged youth turn to the GED. With fewer resources, ABE programs have difficulty serving the needs not only of these youth but of the older drop-outs, such as the Project Hope women, who have been one of their traditional constituencies. In short, current policies seem likely to swell, rather than reduce, the ranks of the undereducated and, hence, the poor.

At the same time as this influx of school failures into the ABE system, especially GED programs, welfare recipients are participating in GED programs at lower rates than before welfare reform because of restrictions on the length of time for completing education or training programs. Access to the lowest levels of adult basic education is increasingly limited for welfare recipients. Recent research by Shaw et al. (2006) confirms widespread "creaming practices . . . when caseworkers pick clients for services on the basis of their perceived ability to complete those services and find work, rather than on their need for increased skills or education" (p. 128). The caseworkers they interviewed said they did more outreach to clients with higher literacy and work skills, and this owed to pressures of accountability. They also manipulated numbers to report more positive outcomes.

As I have shown, under the Workforce Investment Act (WIA) the goals of popular education programs become subsumed in order to help women obtain the GED credential as soon as possible. In a post-welfare society where the labor market is divided into high- and low-paying jobs, a GED is a necessary gatekeeper to further education and better-paying jobs. Studies show that 60 percent of school dropouts eventually earn their GED or other high school credential within twelve years. But although nearly half of GED graduates enroll in postsecondary institutions, fewer than 10 percent finish their degrees (Steinberg, Johnson, and Pennington, 2006).

Hamilton (2002) supports other studies that show welfare-to-work programs can help welfare recipients who have higher literacy skills get their GEDs, but "overall the proportion who earn such a credential is likely to be low. Increases in the proportion of people who obtain a training certificate or postsecondary degree are harder to achieve" (p. 8). We already know that retention rates in ABE are very low because of many of the same barriers that impede successful workforce participation.[4] The "creaming" practices I described in chapter 1 also affect success rates: if caseworkers know that it is unlikely people with very low literacy skills will succeed in education programs, they are likely to require them to do job readiness activities instead of education.[5] Hamilton's (2002) study of Portland, Oregon's "mixed strategy" approach found that

> Decisions about who was not ready to go immediately into job search—and thus who could be initially assigned to education, training, or other activities—were left to program staff, who took into consideration a variety of factors that might affect recipients' employability, including work history, educational attainment, and reading and math skills. GED preparation classes, for example, were offered primarily to people who case managers thought had a good chance of obtaining a GED relatively quickly, and the program indeed raised the proportion of people who received a GED over the five years. In addition, the program led to an increase in the percentage of welfare recipients who received both a GED

> or high school diploma and a trade license or certificate—a combination that non-experimental research has suggested is particularly effective in boosting subsequent earnings. (p. 13)

In Hamilton's study, when the researchers looked at whether the participants in adult basic education programs had made gains in their reading and math test scores, they found that *none* of the programs resulted in higher skills:

> In none of the NEWWS sites in which the standardized reading and math literacy tests were administered two years after study entry did the programs raise test scores, even among people who at study entry wanted or planned to enroll in school. . . . Note, however that most of the programs did not assess welfare recipients for learning disabilities, which could have diminished the programs' ability to improve literacy skills. Some studies have estimated that between one-quarter and one-half of welfare recipients have learning disabilities. (p. 8)

Hamilton also finds that "how long welfare recipients participate in adult education programs can enhance or diminish such programs' beneficial impacts. Overall, the typical participant in an adult education program received the equivalent of about two-thirds of a year of high school instruction" (p. 8). Students who participated in basic education classes for "less than one year did not measurably improve their reading skills" (p. 8). The researchers suggest that "one way to heighten the benefits of education and training would be to retain more students long enough to help them improve their literacy skills and earn a GED and access postsecondary services that would allow them to capitalize on the GED credential" (p. 14). Fass and Garner (2000) looked at studies that investigated the effect of the GED on women's earnings and suggest that "getting a GED has considerable and invaluable impact on recipients' self-esteem, but relatively minor impact on income, unless it is used as a key to entry into further education and training" (Fass and Garner, 2000, p. 42; also see Tyler, Murnane, and Willett, 1999). In other words, these analyses support the original structure and goals of the ALP program.

What Next?

This chapter has shown how difficult—indeed, nearly impossible—it has been for women such as the Project Hope women to raise themselves out of poverty. Clearly, welfare reform has failed them, leaving them uneducated, underemployed, underpaid, and unable to effectively move themselves and their families forward, as they so desperately aspire to do. It would be remiss to end this book without offering an alternative vision for these women. We need to offer them effective educational opportunities, but we also must address the social and economic conditions that continue to shape their lives. In short, we need to:

* increase access to and quality of adult basic literacy classes;
* revoke the Personal Responsibility and Work Opportunity Act, and instead invest resources in providing free access to postsecondary education for all welfare recipients;
* revise the way we calculate the federal poverty standard, increase the minimum wage, and provide more funding for affordable housing, universal child care, and health care programs; and
* create more popular education programs in poor communities.

We need to increase access to and quality of adult basic literacy classes.

Because individual states can implement their own adult education plans under welfare reform and the Workforce Investment Act's "block grant" funding, they have more "flexibility" to shape their own plans, leading to differences among states in terms of how much access there is to adult basic education. Instead of entitlement programs that guarantee rights to social services, federal funding in the form of "block grants" actually decreases funding for social services because the funding remains fixed regardless of whether the population's needs increase. With block grant funding, policymakers can redefine or waive target populations, mandate time limits, and privatize services. A number of advocates suggest that policies under block grants restrict civil rights (Finegold et al., 2004a).

So far, Massachusetts has continued to support basic literacy classes for adults with very low literacy levels, as well as programs that other states do not support, such as correctional educational programs and health literacy programs. The current Massachusetts commissioner for adult education, Robert Bickerton, suggests that the majority of states are not dramatically shifting their funding away from basic literacy:

> There is nothing in WIA that compels a state to reduce its focus to a narrower set of purposes—employment, the pursuit of higher ed, or whatever. The fact is, most states continue to pursue the broad purposes of adult education with and on behalf of our current and future students. This is certainly the case in Massachusetts where there has been no retreat of any kind from those who (in the words of an earlier incarnation of the Adult Education Act) are "least educated and most in need of services." Nor has WIA diminished in any way the breadth

> of providers in Massachusetts who receive support from either federal or state adult education funding. . . . We can be vision driven or we can be law driven—we really must pursue our vision and work like hell to reconcile it with the law—not as difficult to do with WIA as some suggest. (March 6, 2006)

Bickerton closes these remarks: "I never met a student who wanted to stay poor and have bill collectors calling on Saturday mornings. So, I'm not troubled by an emphasis on employment and pursuing higher education—only that these might crowd out the many other important purposes of our AELS." Bickerton's remarks are heartening, but they are not enough.

We need to further investigate the impact of major social policies such as the No Child Left Behind Act, WIA, and the 1996 Personal Responsibility and Work Opportunity Reconciliation Act on the ABE field. In 1998, I participated in a research conference about "The Impact of Welfare Reform on Adult Basic Education" sponsored by the National Center for the Study of Adult Literacy and Learning (NCSALL, 1998). Specifically, the workgroups and speakers discussed the following important questions: "Is there a role for an educational process with undereducated adults that is not employment focused? What changes do adult education programs need to make to support employment as an objective? How is it possible to argue for education as a fundamental right of adults? How do we stop ourselves from becoming 'literacy trainers'? Should adult education be a part of a broad social movement that seeks to increase access to self-sufficiency and opportunity along the lines of class, race, and gender?" (NCSALL, 1998). These questions posed by many of the nation's leading researchers are still relevant today, and should be broadened to examine the connections between K-12 education reform and the ABE field.

We also need to increase public awareness about the growing need for adult literacy. Findings from the 2003 National Assessment of Adult Literacy (NAAL) and the 2003 International Adult Literacy and LifeSkills Survey confirm that in the United States and internationally, individuals with lower literacy skills are more likely to be unemployed or low-income (ProLiteracy, 2006). Nationally, advocates suggest that there is a lack of public knowledge about the diversity of educational and job training programs funded under WIA's Title II. This proved true in Massachusetts in 2002, when the legislature almost shut down the state's system of adult basic education because legislators did not understand the purpose of the ABE line item (Reuys, 2002). Advocates led by the Massachusetts Coalition for Adult Education mobilized an impressive campaign to educate legislators who did not comprehend the scope or delivery of ABE services, and to reinstate funding for ABE. The demand for ABE continues to grow, but funding has not increased to meet the demand (Demetrion, 2005). The National Council of State Directors of Adult Education surveyed WIA-funded programs, in all fifty states, to assess how many people are on waiting lists for ABE services. In the 2005–2006 academic year, there were 93,840 people throughout the United States waiting for publicly funded ABE (Ellison, 2007). The number of people waiting for ABE is likely higher because these figures do not represent numbers of people on waiting lists for programs that do not receive federal or state funding. With more research we can effectively advocate for increasing resources in ABE programs.

We should revoke the Personal Responsibility and Work Opportunity Act and instead invest resources in providing free access to postsecondary education for all welfare recipients.

Recent books by Polakow et al. (2004) and Shaw et al. (2006) examine how welfare reform has restricted access to college for welfare recipients. Kates (1999) argues that the effect of welfare reform on community colleges has been "profound," and "the 15 community colleges of Massachusetts saw enrollment . . . drop by 50 percent on average between 1994 and 1997" (p. 4). Research by Polakow (2003) examined the increasingly limited access to postsecondary education for low-income women in the state of Michigan. It found a pattern of "lawlessness" and "a pattern of widespread disinformation about welfare recipients' rights to benefits, a 'don't ask don't tell' culture in welfare agencies, active discouragement of clients pursuing post-secondary education, and improper cut-offs of childcare subsidies, Medicaid, and food stamps" (p. 2).

State policies toward education and training vary, and Massachusetts has one of the strictest welfare laws in the country (Kates, 1999). In the state of Maine, for instance, completing basic education is a priority, and extensions are granted to allow this to happen. Maine supports a "Parents as Scholars" program to encourage adults to participate in education, including postsecondary education for up to two years; after two years, education may be continued in conjunction with community service and employment (Kates, 1999). Twenty hours of school includes study time and, most important, low-income parents must be allowed to participate if it is unlikely that they can achieve a job that pays 85 percent of the state's median income without more education.

As I argued in chapter 1, access to a postsecondary degree is critical to securing good jobs. Beyond access, we need to provide more college scholarships for low-income students, and invest more in the federal Pell Grant program. In Massachusetts, the One Family Scholars scholarship program is an excellent model of a program that supports low-income women's college education. The One Family scholarship covers costs such as books, child care, and transportation, as well as tuition and fees, and the program offers mentoring and other activities to build a community of scholars. A long-term goal of the federal government should be to provide free higher education at all public colleges and universities. Students at the University of Massachusetts have been working on a campaign for free higher education (see www.freehighered.org) and they seek to pass federal legislation similar to the Servicemen's Readjustment Act of 1944 (commonly known as the G.I. Bill).

We need to revise the way we calculate the federal poverty standard, increase the minimum wage, and provide more funding for affordable housing, universal child care, and health care programs.

As I discussed in chapter 2, the methods used to calculate the federal poverty standard in the United States are seriously flawed because they do not reflect the cost of housing, or regional differences in the cost of living per state. A better measure would be the Family Economic Self-Sufficiency Standard (FESS), a measure that "takes into account the costs of housing, food, transportation, child care, health care, miscellaneous expenses and taxes, and calculates the amount of money it takes for a family to meet basic needs without outside assistance from either the government or family and friends" (Bacon, Russell, and Tighe, 2003, p. 6).

The minimum wage is also a problematic measure for assessing the economic viability of low-income workers. The purchasing power of the federal minimum wage has deteriorated by 20 percent since 1997 (Herbert, 2006). After adjusting for inflation, the value of the minimum wage is at its lowest level since 1955, according to the Economic Policy Institute and the Center for Budget and Policy Priorities. Before Congress voted to raise the minimum wage in January 2007, it had remained unchanged for the longest stretch since it was established in 1938 (Herbert, 2006).

The Deficit Reduction Act of 2005 (Title VII, Subtitle B, Section 7201) includes $200 million in additional child care funding for each year from 2006 to 2010 through the Child Care and Development Block Grant. But these are only matching funds, and, according to the Center for Budget and Policy Priorities, the majority of states will need to increase their child care spending to obtain additional federal funds: "Unfortunately, the additional childcare funding is less than what is needed to ensure that current child care funding keeps pace with inflation and far less than CBO estimates states will need to meet the new work requirements by increasing participation in work activities" (Greenberg and Parrott, 2006, p. 5).

In 2006 the Massachusetts legislature passed a universal health coverage bill, "An Act Providing Access to Affordable, Quality, Accountable Health Care." Other states should increase universal access to health care. In order to address the root causes of homelessness, we need to create more affordable housing and guarantee the "right to housing" (Bratt, Stone, and Hartman, 2006). According to Sard and Springer (2001), "A growing number of studies have found greater welfare reform successes among families with housing assistance than among other low-income families. For example, a Massachusetts study of families leaving welfare found that those with housing subsidies were more likely to be employed 6 to 15 months after leaving welfare than those without subsidies, even though the former group had greater barriers to work" (p. 6). In today's post-welfare society, the focus of social policies is to "encourage good behavior and to connect good behavior with good opportunities" (Traub, 2006). We need social policies that treat poverty as a systemic economic problem, not a problem caused by individuals who make bad choices.

We need to create more popular education programs in poor communities.

In Williams's research on "emerging Popular Education centers" he found that:

> Overall, five significant principles emerge from the discourse on the principles and practices of popular education:
>
> 1) popular education is committed to the self-determination and emancipation of subordinated groups within society;
> 2) people are to be seen as self-conscious political actors capable of changing themselves and the social structure;
> 3) loyalties are developed and maintained in terms of people, not institutions;
> 4) the endeavor of popular education is to learn to critically analyze individual and collective experiences in conjunction with participatory social action and to build on and transform these analyzed experiences in a critical way towards progressive social change;

5) popular education is about facilitating learning through practice based on peer teaching in which all persons involved learn with and from each other. (1996: 105)

The ABE field needs more popular education programs that follow these principles. Sticht (1999) studied how American adult educators view their work by looking at the "dominant metaphors and analogies" they use to describe their role as teachers working with adult learners (Speights, 2001, pp. 18–19). The survey found that the most popular metaphor American adult basic education teachers used to describe their work was psychotherapy. Sticht notes that "interestingly, the revolutionary metaphor, which might be associated with social justice and the critical literacy movement, especially the work of Paulo Freire, did not emerge in the top three metaphors or analogies thought appropriate for adult literacy education" (quoted in Speights, 2001, p. 19). Many adult educators "view depression rather than oppression as a more serious problem to be overcome" (quoted in Speights, 2001, p. 19). These findings are not surprising, given the hegemony of neoliberalism that permeates social services for the poor. As I noted in chapter 1, such medicalization metaphors dominate the policies and practices of neoliberal social welfare policies (Lyon-Callo, 2004).

Within this political context, popular education is a challenge. According to Heaney (1996):

> Attempts to adapt the work of Freire for the most part occurred in the context of adult basic education programs (literacy, English-as-a-Second-Language, GED preparation, adult high schools) and have therefore faced head-on the structural limitations of schooling. . . . The schooling model imposed by federal and state agencies that provide most of the funding for adult basic education frequently mandated a narrow, instrumental curriculum. . . . Freire-inspired projects, no matter how grounded in the local community, have always found themselves at risk in the competition for funding. In the name of accountability, funding sources exert control and claim ownership. (Heaney, 1996, p. 36)

I agree with Bee (1993), who calls for a critical approach to women's literacy and argues for using "reading and writing as a means for enabling women who have been conditioned to accept second-class status to affirm their aspirations as valid and their knowledge and views of life as genuine contributions to the net stock of human understanding. Merely enabling women to read and write without reference to their social and political inequality and its origins contributes materially to maintaining their oppression" (p. 106). She argues that women's literacy programs that focus on improving self-esteem or building confidence are problematic because:

> unless such programs also contain opportunities for women to critically analyze the social causes for so many of them lacking confidence in their own abilities—and especially the relationship between this state of mind and women's social conditioning within family, education, religions, and the state—there is little chance of women moving beyond enhanced personal attitudes to a deeper awareness of the need for structural change if women are collectively to achieve genuine and lasting equality of opportunity. (p. 106)

Programs such as Project Hope's Adult Learners Program have the potential to create genuine and lasting social change.

Conclusion

On July 21, 2006, the Project Hope staff moved into a beautiful $5.4 million building on Dudley Street. The new Project Hope "headquarters" was a long-awaited dream for Sister Margaret and her staff, as well as the Dudley community. The environmentally friendly, four-story building represents a positive future for Project Hope. The organization has increased its staff and doubled the number of families it serves through its programs. The new facility offers a community computer center, career training programs, and ESOL classes for neighborhood immigrants. Other community programs are currently being developed. The expansion of the Adult Learners Program (ALP) has been one of Project Hope's most impressive accomplishments, demonstrating its continued mission to address the great need for adult literacy education in the Dudley community.

However, in the post-welfare era, the pressures of accountability, efficiency, and self-sufficiency erode the goals of popular education programs such as the ALP. In order to maintain federal and state education funding, the ALP faces increasing pressure to produce more GED graduates per year, to move students into employment more quickly, and to demonstrate improvements in learning gains by using standardized tests (such as REEP or BEST). If a student drops out, another student must fill that "slot" immediately. Teachers are teaching more classes and doing more counseling as the women are younger and have greater needs. As one teacher, Carol, explained, "The women today are hard-core poor." Yet we have just seen that such women need the most support and are least likely to be helped by welfare reform policies and practices. Indeed, they are in even greater need of the comprehensive and empowering education that the ALP was originally designed to offer.

In the post-welfare era, Project Hope's ALP and other popular education programs face an uncertain future. Sister Lois explained that during welfare reform debates she "always felt a very important question was being disregarded, and almost like not there, and the question was: 'Who is an educated person?'" She told me, "let's really try to get to the root of what that honestly means, for ourselves as teachers, but also for students to understand, what goes into being an educated person? Because we have all kinds of messages about that from outside ourselves, and the internalized oppression coming from that place, too."

Carol, a teacher quoted earlier, powerfully characterizes what is needed in women's literacy programs everywhere:

> I believe that you can know how to read, write, and do math, which we're teaching the women, and they are making strides, but how many women drop out? Where do they go after they get this? Because they get these subjects and get their GED, what then happens to them? And so, without a good sense of self esteem, without having health literacy, and without having strategies that will take them beyond the GED, because we feel that they're not just "some people," the GED isn't gonna even probably be honored, or what can you really get with the GED? So what we feel now is that this is the foundation, okay? Because these women are becoming so strong, their self-esteem, their sense of worthiness, their sense of value is what's gonna carry them through to life-long learning. And, the thing that I want them to know is they can have more than a GED, and they start looking towards the future. They come and they're thinking like, "I just want that great American dream," which I say a little sarcastically, to get their GED, but then we get their appetites whet, and they start thinking about everything, other things. Like Naomi, who is sixty-five and wants to be a lawyer. We say, "Go for it." You know? Women who want to come in and they want to be a CNA [certified nursing assistant] now they want to be a nurse. So really opening them up to see that they can have more because of what they've been exposed to here.

In previous chapters, I explored how the popular education classes at Project Hope's Adult Learners Program promoted a "critical consciousness" among learners. Through generative themes and codes, the women developed a critical awareness regarding their shared experiences and interests. Their growing understanding of their relationship to others, and to the society they live in, lessened their self-blame. Through popular education, the Project Hope women's "cultures of silence" were broken as they came to understand how their individual problems were connected to social problems (Freire, 1990). Sister Lois feels that the ALP's popular education classes allowed women the opportunity to reflect on their place in the world, to understand how the economy works, to challenge their internalized oppression, to bond with other women, and to build community. All of this, she points out, can be "very threatening" to the status quo:

> We keep women so busy that they do not have time to process anything, and particularly low-income women who are trying to juggle many things, you can keep people so busy. And I often feel that's a conspiracy. I really do. . . . It's really a desirable thing for a culture that is as dominated by males and by whites, really, to not want people to have time to really find themselves. Do you know what I mean? It goes against the whole economic system. And isn't it scary? Because when people do have that time [to process things], then they begin to get connected with other people and, oh my gosh, they, they're going to organize. This is very threatening to the status quo. Very threatening.

Another teacher, Agnes, agreed: "And [the women] don't need as much. It's like, you don't get into that consumer mentality . . . you know. If you have a sense of yourself, what do you need? Not a lot. And so it [popular education] goes totally against the system that had you always needing, always consuming, always looking outside yourself."

For the teachers and learners at Project Hope, neither the GED nor "any job" is a sufficient end. To truly overcome poverty, they believe, we must both pay attention to the means and overcome social injustice. Popular education is crucial to both these tasks. In the United States we have enough resources available to provide literacy services to everyone who wants the opportunity to further their education. The neoliberal discourses that define the primary purposes of literacy in market terms and as "worker training" fail to address the unequal socioeconomic conditions that create the need for literacy, and thus they have failed the women of Project Hope.

Epilogue: An Unfinished Conversation

In the fall of 1996, I arranged for a group of women from Project Hope to be guest speakers in a sociology class I was teaching at Northeastern University (NU). My college students were studying welfare reform and many of them were at best apathetic and at worst prejudiced toward the plight of poor people. The American students in the class believed wholeheartedly that the United States is a meritocracy: if an individual works hard, he or she will achieve great success. I hoped that the opportunity to have a discussion with "real" welfare recipients might challenge their hegemonic beliefs about meritocracy in the United States and help them see how social forces limit opportunities for certain groups of people, no matter how hard they work. Still, I was nervous about how the college students would react to the women's stories.

On the day of our trip to the university, Florence, Yvette, Leticia, Cynthia, Delila, Susan, Georgia, and Tashawna were excited, nervous, and a little self-conscious. I noticed the women had styled their hair and were wearing their finest clothes. Although the Greater Boston area has the world's highest concentration of universities and colleges, only Florence had ever visited a college campus before. As the women walked around the campus, carrying their book bags, they joked to Sister Lois: "We look like college students!" When we entered the classroom, the NU students watched the Project Hope women as they sat down at the front of the room. I introduced them, explaining that they were full-time students and mothers. The women talked about why they ended up on welfare, why they wanted to get off welfare, their hopes for achieving their GEDs, the obstacles they faced as they attempted to finish school, and what they hoped their children would accomplish in the future.

After the women spoke, a couple of students asked them questions that were quite critical and insensitive. One student, apparently forgetting that the women had children, asked why they did not consider becoming roommates and renting an apartment together, because, after all, "wouldn't that be better than living in a shelter?" Another student said he was impressed by their motivation and praised them for being more motivated than "other welfare recipients." A few of his peers nodded their heads in agreement. For the mostly upper- and middle-class white college students, the hard-working, ambitious, education-minded Project Hope women were the opposite of what they had expected. When the women did not fit the stereotypes they imagined, the students decided that they were exceptions, not "normal" welfare recipients.

One white male student's written reflection expresses these conflicting images and messages:

> It's really too bad that the welfare system makes it so hard for people to improve their lives. Not only is the money not enough to pay the bills and buy food, but being forced to volunteer or work in oppressive jobs is not effective. I admit that at one time I would think that this [welfare reform] is a good idea. Now I hear these stories of these women getting their education but being forced to put it aside, it's crazy. On the other hand, there are people who are not self-motivated and do nothing all day. I think this would be put down as a stereotype in our class if someone had said it. Or it would be defended by someone saying that they have no choice that they're stuck on that couch by society.

This student's contradictory feelings were shared by many of his classmates. He is conflicted about welfare reform because he believes it is wrong to force people to give up on their education. However, the powerful neoliberal ideology of individual "choice" frames this young man's belief that many welfare recipients "do nothing all day" and are poor because they do not have a strong work ethic. He further dismisses sociological explanations for the women's problems by mocking the notion that the women are "stuck on that couch by society."

Another young white woman suggested that welfare was "not fair," but "sometimes you have to make sacrifices. I don't think that anyone should have to give up going to school, but if it comes down to that, they should try to do both school and Community Service. When I asked the question [to the women] yesterday, 'Why can't you go to school and do Community service?,' I did not mean to offend anyone, I just felt that even though [welfare reform is] not fair, sometimes you have to make sacrifices that will pay off in the end." In their reflection papers, my college students overwhelmingly felt that the homeless women's stories were powerful, but that they did not represent the "norm." The women's attempts to "better themselves" did not challenge their stereotypes, but instead supported the dominant neoliberal ideology about personal responsibility—these homeless women were fulfilling the ideal of personal responsibility. Though these college students were experiencing a profound disconnect between ideology and reality, they worked hard to reconnect the stereotypes in their minds with what they saw in front of them.

The next day, when I spoke with the Project Hope women, they said they were moved by the experience, but unsettled by the different perspectives they encountered. The women were surprised that only two students, out of the class of forty, were African American. Susan commented that a number of the students "turned red" when they were talking and she could tell they were uncomfortable because "it is easy to see when white people are mad." Delila said, "Not all of the students believed what we said, but a lot of them did try to understand and asked questions. We just gave them a piece of information about our lives. But, that piece of information is not enough to believe in and to accept it as real." Similarly, Florence pointed out, "A lot of the kids in the class didn't think that it was real, what we were saying . . . about what we go through as adult learners." Yvette observed:

> Going to Northeastern was quite an experience because not everybody there had the same perspective. We was thinking different about them and they was thinking different about us. I never been in a room where I thought that those people up there were better than me and that was the situation that I was kind of feeling when I was there. You know? They're in college, they're more than us, they know more than us. But it wasn't even like that. They didn't even have a slight idea of what real life was all about. . . . College is a dream to them. We're not having a dream. We live in real life. We out there struggling everyday for our kids, for ourselves. People looking at us like, "If we could do it, you could do it." It seemed to me that they thought our life was an excuse, because we kept saying, "Well, we have kids . . ."

I also shared some of the NU students' reflection papers with the Project Hope women, especially the paper written by the only African American male:

> I think it is so important for us as students who are "studying" people, analyzing and trying to explain why people are the way they are, to

> not forget to ask those people themselves. How can we say that we are learning about a group of people if we cannot even talk to them and see their perspective? . . . I thought it was interesting the way my classmates looked while these women were speaking. It was almost as if you could see people thinking—"Yeah, that's too bad, but maybe if you tried a little harder, if you weren't so lazy, then maybe . . ." I hope these women's stories had an effect on the class, on their views and their feelings about change.

Yvette and Susan wanted to continue the discussion with the Northeastern students. Susan said, "I was surprised that there's college students that don't know about a support system that can be good and can be abusive. We should go back because it takes times to talk out freely. It takes time to speak out about the welfare system." Yvette added:

> If we get a chance to go back, maybe we could tell them what the GED is all about. We're not gonna get the GED and sit down. I wanna go to college, further my education, have my electrician's certificate. If I was to be there [at Northeastern University] longer, I'm quite sure that they would have got a different perspective of how we are living. It wouldn't have been an issue that it was "an excuse," it would have been more like, "Wow, they've been through a lot and they still going. These are strong womans." Not, "These womans are weak, they coming up with excuses, they got all these bunch of kids." They were trying to blame us.

After hearing the women's stories, a number of my Northeastern students said they had changed their feelings and attitudes toward women on welfare. A few students thanked the women for presenting a "real" picture of what it is like to live in poverty. Still, as Yvette stated in the previous quote, the Project Hope women wondered who was living a "real" life, the college students or them?

Sister Lois described the class visit as an "unfinished conversation." One of the students recommended that those who are studying about the poor should "ask" and learn from the people most affected by poverty. Yvette agreed and wished she had been there "longer," because if they had more time, they could have changed the Northeastern students' thinking about welfare recipients. I hope that this book continues that "unfinished conversation," and that readers will be moved by these stories to advocate for policies that increase access to education at all levels and guarantee a right to literacy and a route out of poverty for everyone.

APPENDIX: NOTES ON METHODOLOGY

> The core of critical ethnography is the study of the process of domestication and social entrapment by which we are made content with our life conditions.
>
> —Thomas, 1993, p. 7

In an ethnographic study, a researcher collects information by observing and interviewing living members of a group and examining the available written documents from and about that group (Zaharlick, 1992). In brief, the basics of ethnographic research include: a) developing relationships with people so that information can be exchanged; b) assuming the perspective of the group being studied; c) learning about the group over an extended period of time and through firsthand observation; and d) using multiple data collection techniques (Zaharlick, 1992). Ethnographers try to gain an insider's perspective on how people create meaning, which involves understanding the dominant ideology of the group (Thomas, 1993). In addition, the ethnographer's desire to learn from insiders requires a "holistic orientation" which, according to Fetterman (1989), "demands a great deal of time in the field to gather the many kinds of data that together create a picture of the social whole. It also requires multiple methods and multiple hypotheses to ensure that the researcher covers all angles" (p. 29). Critical ethnographers are especially concerned with the effects of the researcher on the researched and vice versa. According to Thomas (1993), "The researcher is part and parcel of the research process, and we must always be aware not only of how we might influence and shape the slice of culture we study, but also of how we ourselves are changed by the research process" (67).[1] Despite this caveat, the descriptive data gathered in ethnographic fieldwork provides a rich understanding of a social group's ways of life.

In order to develop a comprehensive ethnographic study of the low-income women who participated in the Adult Learners Program at Project Hope, I used multiple research methods including education histories, participant observation, interviews, focus groups, and text analysis of program/agency data.

Profile of Sample

Each of the fifty women in this study participated in the ALP for at least three months and up to three years. The majority of the women were African American and Puerto Rican. Specifically, twenty women were African American, eleven were Puerto Rican, six were Haitian, three were from Trinidad, two were from Barbados, and two identified themselves as "bi-racial." There was one woman each from Jamaica, St. Vincent, Cape Verde, a nation in Africa, and Honduras, and one woman was Irish American. The average age of the women at the time interviews were conducted was thirty, with a range of twenty-one to forty-seven. The average number of children was two, with a range of one to five. Eighty percent of the women received AFDC/TANF welfare benefits at least some of the time between 1995 and 1998. Of the remaining 20 percent, three received Supplemental Security Income (SSI), four worked part-time, and three had no income at all. Sixty-six percent of the women had participated in the paid labor force at some point.

Forty-two percent of the women in the study were homeless for at least three months between 1995 and 1998. The other 58 percent had been homeless between 1990 and 1995, and were still considered to be "at risk" of homelessness. The majority of the formerly homeless women were involved in shelter follow-up programs that had referred them to the ALP.

Most of the women quit school at the tenth grade, but some left as early as seventh grade and seven women never attended school at all. The women's reading comprehension levels varied: 28 percent had reading comprehension levels ranging from zero to fourth grade, 46 percent had reading levels between fifth and eight grade, and 26 percent had reading levels between ninth and twelfth grade. Eighty-two percent of the women had attended at least one other adult education program prior to enrolling in the ALP.

Gathering Information in the Field

As I mentioned in the introductory chapter, I first visited Project Hope as an adjunct faculty member at Northeastern University seeking to establish community service opportunities for Northeastern students. From January 1995 through June 1997, I was an unpaid volunteer in the Adult Learners Program ten to fifteen hours per week. In July 1997, I was hired to teach Social Studies for ten hours a week. After I completed my data collection in 1998, I was hired full-time to coordinate the ALP and worked in this capacity until June 2000. From 2000–2006, I volunteered for the ALP, providing training to teachers, co-teaching health literacy classes, guest lecturing for special events, and consulting with teachers and staff on special projects such as the Women in Community Development program, the One Family Scholars program, and the Women, Violence, Adult Education project.

Working at Project Hope exposed me to the many social services provided by the agency and increased my knowledge of public policies affecting the organization, its homeless families, and the Dudley community. As the ALP coordinator, I attended many meetings and conferences sponsored by the Massachusetts Department of Education's Adult and Community Learning Services (e.g., Directors' Council, Adult Education for Homeless network, ABE Health, ACLS Community Planning). I also participated in various coalitions and advocacy groups related to ABE and welfare reform in Massachusetts.

I conducted all of my research, except for the follow-up interviews, between April 1995 and January 1998.

Participant Observation

Between April 1995 and January 1998, I conducted ethnographic research as a participant observer with the fifty women in various settings including, but not limited to, visits in their homes, appointments at welfare offices, and special occasions such as birthday parties and cookouts. I also spent more than 1,500 hours as a participant observer in adult literacy classes. The classes I observed included social studies, science, literature and arts, math, writing, economic literacy and a consciousness raising/community building course called "Loves Herself, Regardless." My class observations focused on subject matter, curriculum resources and materials, student writings, and interactions among teachers and students.

In addition, I participated in all ALP faculty meetings, retreats, and celebrations. To gain an understanding of the most pressing issues in the literacy field and the role of the ALP in the context of the broader community, I also conducted participant observation in adult literacy coalitions in Boston's Roxbury and Dorchester neighborhoods and observed meetings at a variety of Boston-area social service agencies.

Education Histories

The women's educational histories were a crucial piece of data for this study. Each woman completed an education history within three months after enrolling in the ALP. I received permission to obtain copies of the educational histories, which were all handwritten. The education history questionnaire was adapted from Campolo (1995) and addressed some of the following questions: What schools did you attend? Do you remember if there were any stressful family, friend, or work situations that occurred while you were going to school? If so, how do you think these stressful situations affected your learning? When you were growing up did you see family members reading? Did you have any serious health problems that kept you out of school? When you were in school did you receive any special awards? What things made you feel proud? What things were you not proud of? What was your most stressful school experience? What was your best school experience? Were you ever placed in a special education class or an advanced class? Were you ever told you had a learning disability? Why did you quit school? What do you remember about the day you quit? What conversations did you have with your parents, relatives, friends, teachers, counselors, yourself? What factors led to your decision to return to school to finish your GED? Did you attend any other GED or ABE programs? Who (or what) is supportive of your efforts to finish your education? Who (or what) presents a challenge? What are your goals for the next year? Where do you see yourself five years from now?

Text Analysis

I collected a variety of documents for text analysis, including women's writings from classroom assignments and projects, student assessments, teacher lesson plans, publications by ALP teachers, annual reports to funders, strategic planning reports, photographs, videos, newsletters, press clippings, and archival data about Project Hope.

Focus Groups

In the summer of 1996, I conducted four focus groups with homeless women and teachers in the ALP. The first focus group consisted of seven women who were currently enrolled in classes. A second focus group, in August, comprised ten women who would be starting classes in September. The third and fourth focus groups included six ALP teachers. The focus groups ranged in duration from an hour and a half to three hours. They were tape-recorded and transcribed. The program coordinator assisted in the facilitation of two student focus groups, which enabled me to record observations during the discussions. The questions used for the focus groups were adapted from the education history questionnaire and developed in collaboration with the program coordinator and the curriculum coordinator. Some of the questions asked in the focus groups included: What were the reasons you dropped out of school? When did you first consider returning to school? Why did you come to the ALP? Did you attend any other adult education programs before the ALP? What are some obstacles you have faced since you returned to school? Describe your experience at the ALP. What are the expectations put on you by teachers and other adult learners? What do you expect from the ALP? How would you describe yourself as a learner? How do you learn best? What kinds of things do you enjoy learning? Where do you get the support you need to keep on learning? What is the biggest challenge for you now as an adult learner?

Interviews

Between April 1995 and January 1998, I conducted in-depth interviews with twenty-five homeless and formerly homeless women, seven ALP teachers, six Project Hope and ALP staff members, and ten community leaders. The majority of interviews were tape-recorded; however, four women did not want to be tape-recorded, so I just took written notes.

Between September 2003 and June 2005, I conducted follow-up interviews with fifteen women who participated in the ALP between 1995 and 1998. I also collected data (some of it incomplete) from another ten women. All follow-up interviews ranged from an hour and a half to three hours in length.

The purpose of the follow-up interviews was to examine the impact of the GED and welfare reform on the women's lives. Some of the questions asked in the follow-up interview included: What sections of the GED tests were most challenging for you? What do you remember about the day you passed the GED? What impact did your GED have on other people in your life? Do you think you could have done what you are doing now without your GED? What obstacles were you facing that made it necessary for you to be on welfare? How did welfare help you? What was hard about it? What were the most important things you learned from your experience with the welfare system? How do you feel about your health/physical condition? Do you have health insurance? Do you work outside the home? Full-time or part-time? If yes, how do you feel about your job? How do you feel about your current housing situation? How do you feel about your financial situation? What is your opinion about the community where you live? Are you active in community organizations such as church, parent teacher organizations (PTOs), cultural groups, sports groups, or other volunteer work? Did you vote in the last election? Why or why not?

Interpretation of the Data

As I have just outlined, over ten years I collected a significant amount of data. As I developed the narrative and analysis that make up this book, I repeatedly read over field notes, education histories, the women's writings, and transcripts from interviews and focus groups. I looked for "frequencies" in what the women were saying and I examined whether there was an order, or "process," that led to a particular action or event (Lofland and Lofland, 1995). I also cross-referenced focus group and interview data from the same women as a way of conducting "consistency checks" (Carspecken, 1996, p. 166). For example, transcripts occasionally revealed inconsistencies between what a woman said in an individual interview and what she shared in a focus group. My methods for analyzing the data were influenced by the interpretive methods of Way (1998) who uses case studies "to present the regularity and texture of everyday living" (p. 41).

Using spreadsheets, I organized recurring themes into "conceptual" categories. Specifically, I worked with three broad categories: "School life," "Family life," and "Community life." Under the category of "School life," I examined the women's educational histories; under the category of "Family life," I analyzed the poverty-related obstacles in their lives; and, under the category of "Community life," I explored how the women related to one another within the context of the ALP, as well as their developing critical consciousness as a result of popular education.

Build an Alternative Education, Training, and Jobs Program For Women on Welfare

⇓ *The new Welfare Regulations will restrict educational and training opportunities for women!*

⇓ *The new Welfare Regulations will stop you from getting skills you need to get viable jobs!*

⇓ *The new Welfare Regulations will force women to do unpaid work which will depress wages, benefits and working conditions for all workers!*

Women on Welfare and Agencies
Come on Tuesday, May 21 from 10 am to noon
to Alexander/Magnolia Coop Center,
36 Alexander Street in Dorchester

For more information please call: Ruth Rubalcava at 442-1880 or Sheree Jemmott at 983-9677

NOTES

Introduction

1. D'Amico (2004) notes: "People of color are disproportionately represented among those both in literacy programs and in need of literacy when compared to their representation in the population as a whole" (pp. 21–22).

2. According to Kates (2004), "Several studies referred to families that returned to welfare as recidivists, a term typically used to refer to repeat criminals" (p. 32).

3. Devine (1994) argues, "While it may be acquired by most members of a culture, and hence be regarded as a characteristic of that culture, literacy thus envisioned is a personal quality of the individual. It is, furthermore, a static quality: Literacy skills, once attained, become part of the individual's permanent repertoire" (p. 223).

4. In Quigley's history of the National Literacy Act legislation (1997), he notes that "the references to goals and potential were additions that were vigorously fought for by a small number of adult literacy educators who had been invited to advise the political decision makers on 'what literacy is'" (p. 14).

5. Sticht (2002) states: "Of the more than 31 million enrollees in the AELS from 1992 to 1999, 7.9 million were the working poor, more than 3.3 million were welfare recipients, 9.3 million were unemployed, and 2.2.million were incarcerated. More than two-thirds of the 15 million enrollees during 1992–1996 had not completed twelve years of education or received a high school diploma, and more than 3.4 million were immigrants" (p. 10; also see National Center for Education Statistics, 2000).

Chapter 1: Framing the Blame and Gain

1. The Adult Education field includes educational programs such as English for Speakers of Other Languages (ESOL), General Education Diploma (GED), Family Literacy, Prison Literacy, Workplace Literacy, and Adult Basic Literacy (ABE). These programs have different goals and serve diverse populations.

2. Katz (1995) writes, "The mass production of clocks and watches began at about the same time as the mass production of public schools" (p. 108). During welfare reform debates, Governor Kirk Fordice of Mississippi said, "the only job training that welfare recipients need is a good alarm clock" (Abramovitz, 1996, p. 28).

3. Globalization "means that global corporations and elites will seek 'unrestrained' access to the world's markets and maximum profits. It means the end of

the welfare state and an increase in police and military power and repression. It means the downsizing and privatization of government services." Furthermore, globalization means "widening gaps between wealth and poverty (the average worker earned $517 per week last year, while the average CEO [in the United States] earned $155,769 a week); the end of social welfare and entitlement programs; public education is privatized; violence and incarceration rates increase; and, environmental degradation" (Project South, 2002, p. 1). According to Hallgren and Weiner (2003), "Globalization encompasses a number of factors including the collapse of old post–World War II order; the loss of power of the nation-state to the transnational corporation; and the use of communication and technology to transact business (and process knowledge) across national and continental boundaries. Globalization is seen by some as a new freedom but by others as the 'new world disorder' where no one seems now to be in control" (p. 317; see also Castells, 2000).

4. In 2003, more than two-thirds of Massachusetts jobs were concentrated in education and health services (18 percent of non-farm employment), wholesale and retail trade (15.3 percent), professional and business services (13.7 percent), government (13.1 percent), and manufacturing (10.2 percent) (see Massachusetts Budget and Policy Center, *The state of working Massachusetts 2004*).

5. Adult education is defined in the act as "services or instruction below the postsecondary level for individuals who have attained 16 years of age; who are not enrolled or required to be enrolled in secondary school under state law; and who lack sufficient mastery of basic educational skills to enable the individuals to function effectively in society; who do not have a secondary school diploma or its recognized equivalent, and have not achieved an equivalent level of education; or, who are unable to read, speak, or write the English language" (Murphy, 2003, p. 3).

Chapter 2: Hope on Magnolia Street

1. The history of DSNI is documented in the book *Streets of Hope: The Fall and Rise of an Urban Neighborhood* by Peter Medoff and Holly Sklar (1994), as well as in the documentary *Holding Ground,* produced by Leah Mahan.

2. According to Bachtel (1999), "In the first year, $550 million was divided among 50 states to fund education for adults who were homeless. Almost 18,000 people participated in AEH in the first year. Funding for programs was later restricted based on 'success' and other evaluative criteria. Still, over the eight-year period, more than 150,000 adults participated" (p. 10). In 1996, the federal budget for McKinney homeless assistance programs was cut by 27 percent, and funding was completely eliminated for the Adult Education for the Homeless program. In 1998, the Workforce Investment Act repealed the Job Training for the Homeless, and consolidated more than fifty employment, training, and literacy programs. The McKinney Act is now focused on educating homeless children (USDOE, 1998; Sperazi, 1990).

Chapter 3: Mothering in the War Years

1. Although rent control laws existed in only a few cities, such as Boston, in 1996, Massachusetts voters passed a statewide referendum ending "rent control"

(see University of Massachusetts [1998] report: *A Profile of Housing in Massachusetts*).

2. According to Smythe and Isserlis (2003), "feminist historians have shown that during times of rapid social and economic change, the competency of mothers has been a concern for the government of the day" (p. 28).

3. Hayes (1992) and Hayes and Smith (1994) examined publications about women in the major adult education journals. Several themes (or perspectives) emerged that perpetuated dominant assumptions about women in adult education. The majority of the articles they analyzed lacked "attention to the significance of gender in women's lives," and there was an "individualistic orientation" that ignored "how the process or content of women's learning might be related to gender-related social norms" (1994, p. 213). They also found that racial, cultural, and class differences in women's experiences were unrecognized, because much of the research focused on white middle-class women who participate in adult education classes.

Chapter 4: Around the Round Table

1. See C. Mouffe, ed. (1979) *Gramsci and Marxist Theory* for a more detailed analysis of hegemony.

2. Popular education's roots can be found in Brazil in the late 1950s and early 1960s during a period of political reform, industrialization, and great social changes (Ferreira and Ferreira, 1997). This period also corresponded to Pope John XXIII's initiation of "progressive" changes in the Catholic Church that inspired political activity among Catholics.

Chapter 5: Women of Strength

1. For an excellent discussion about "common sense" knowledge, see Wendy Luttrell's (1997) *Schoolsmart and Motherwise: Working-class Women's Identity and Schooling.*

2. Beder's (1999) "Outcomes and Impacts Study" examined outcome and impact studies conducted since the late 1960s, including national studies, state-level studies, and studies of welfare, workplace, and family literacy programs.

Chapter 6: Laboring to Learn, Learning to Labor

1. Transitional Assistance for Needy Families (TANF), replaced Aid to Families with Dependent Children (AFDC). See Withorn (1999).

2. The programs in this study were running under the federal Family Support Act of 1988 when the FSA required the government to provide education, employment, and support services to adults receiving AFDC. AFDC recipients had to participate in the FSA's Job Opportunities and Basic Skills (JOBS) Training programs. When the PRWORA passed in 1996, these programs continued to operate (Hamilton, 2002, p. 2).

3. This study's methodology included random assignment research design of eleven programs at seven sites, N=40,000.

4. According to a study in Massachusetts, 20 percent of adult learners drop out after a month. A number of studies find that 50 percent of the adults who enroll in ABE classes drop out before completing ten weeks of instruction (Young et al., 1994; Comings et al., 1999).

5. See Hays (2003) for a critique of "caseworker discretion" and the impact of caseworkers on welfare recipients (p. 86).

Appendix

1. I explore these issues in more detail in "Multiple Identities & Shifting Boundaries," a paper coauthored with Shobha Hamal-Gurung (Hamal-Gurung and Rivera, 2003).

REFERENCES

Abramovitz, M. (1996). *Under attack, fighting back: Women and welfare in the United States.* New York: Monthly Review Press.

Albelda, R. (1998, November 22). Off the welfare rolls to where? *Boston Globe,* p. E3.

Albelda, R., & Tilly, C. (1997). *Glass ceilings and bottomless pits: Women's work, women's poverty.* Boston: South End Press.

Albelda, R. A., Withorn, A., & Navin, C. (1998). *Poor timing: An analysis of Massachusetts' welfare time limits.* Boston: Boston Area Academics Working Group on Poverty, University of Massachusetts-Boston.

Allard, M. A., Colten, M. E., Albelda, R., & Cosenza, C. (1997). *In harm's way? Domestic violence, AFDC receipt, and welfare reform in Massachusetts.* Boston: McCormack Institute, Center for Survey Research, University of Massachusetts-Boston.

Althusser, L. (1971). Ideology and ideological state apparatuses. *Lenin and philosophy.* New York: Monthly Review Press.

Anderson, G. (1989). Critical ethnography in education: Origins, current status, and new directions. *Review of Educational Research, 59,* (3), 249–70.

Andreola, B. A. (1993). Action, knowledge and reality in the educational work of Paulo Freire. *Educational Action Research, 1,* (2), 221–34.

Antola-Robinson, H. (1994). *The ethnography of empowerment: The transformative power of classroom interaction.* Washington, D.C.: The Falmer Press.

Anyon, J. (1997). *Ghetto schooling: A political economy of urban educational reform.* New York: Teachers College Press.

Apple, M. W. (1996). *Cultural politics and education.* New York: Teachers College Press.

Apple, M. W. (1999). Rhetorical reforms: Markets, standards and inequality. *Current Issues in Comparative Education, 1,* (2), 1–13.

Apple, M. W. (2004). Between good sense and bad sense: Race, class, and learning from Learning to Labor. In Dolby, N., Dimitriadis, G., & Willis, P. (Eds.), *Learning to labor in new times.* New York: Routledge.

Arenson, K. W. (2004, May 15). More youths opt for GED, skirting high-school hurdle. *New York Times.*

Arenson, K. W. (2004, June 16). Making GED programs more than test prep. *New York Times.*

Arenson, K. W. (2006, May 30). Can't complete high school? Go right to college. *New York Times.*

Aronowitz, S. (1977). Preface to the Morningside edition. In P. Willis, *Learning to labor: how working class kids get working class jobs.* New York: Columbia University Press.

Aronowitz, S., & Giroux, H. A. (1993). *Education still under siege* (2nd ed.) Westport, Conn.: Bergin & Garvey.

Association for Community-Based Education. (1988). *Literacy for empowerment: A resource handbook for adult educators.* Washington, D.C.: Author.

Aucoin, D. (1994, February 16). Roxbury case cited in welfare debate Democrats, Republicans say their reform plans would have prevented abuse. *Boston Globe,* Metro, pp. 19–21.

Aucoin, D. (1994, July 30). New consensus is emerging on welfare reform. *Boston Globe.*

Auerbach, E. (1989). Toward a socio-contextual approach to family literacy. *Harvard Educational Review, 59,* (2), 165–91.

Auerbach, E. (1992). Making meaning, making change: Participatory curriculum development for adult ESL literacy. Washington, D.C.: Delta Systems.

Bachtel, E. (1999). *Servicing adult homeless learners: A guide for ABE administrators, educators, and counselors.* Boston: Systems for Adult Basic Education, Massachusetts Department of Education.

Bacon, J., & Russell, L. H. (2005). *Dudley families first: A framework for economic self-sufficiency.* Boston: The Women's Educational Industrial Union.

Bacon, J., Russell, L. H., & Tighe, J. (2003). *The self-sufficiency standard: Where Dudley area families stand.* Boston: Mass Fess Project, Women's Educational Industrial Union.

Balliro, L. (2004). Adult secondary education in Massachusetts: Options and issues. *Field Notes, 13,* (4), 9–15.

Barnicle, M. (1994, October 6). Ventura failed to be a symbol. *Boston Globe,* Metro, pp. 33–36.

Barton, P. (2005). *One-Third of a nation: Rising dropout rates and declining opportunities.* Princeton, N.J.: Educational Testing Service.

Bassuk, E. L. (1990). Who are homeless families? Characteristics of sheltered mothers and children. *Community Mental Health Journal, 26,* (5), 425–34.

Bauman, Z. (1998). *Work, consumerism, and the new poor.* Buckingham, Eng.: Open University Press.

Bee, B. (1993). Critical literacy and the politics of gender. In C. Lankshear & P. McLaren (Eds.), *Critical literacy: Politics, praxis, and the postmodern.* Albany: State University of New York Press.

Beder, H. (1987). Dominant paradigms, adult education, and social justice. *Adult Education Quarterly, 37,* (2), 105–13.

Beder, H. (1991). The stigma of illiteracy. *Adult Basic Education, 1,* (2), 67–78.

Beder, H. (1996). Popular education: An appropriate educational strategy for community-based organizations. *New Directions for Adult & Continuing Education, 70,* 73–83.

Beder, H. (1998). Lessons from NCSALL's outcomes and impacts study. *Focus on Basics, 2,* (D), 1–8.

Beder, H. (1999). *The outcomes and impacts of adult literacy education in the United States.* Cambridge, Mass.: National Center for the Study of Adult Learning and Literacy, Harvard University.

Beder, H., & Valentine, T. (1990). Motivational profiles of adult basic education students. *Adult Education Quarterly, 40,* (2), 78–94.

Benmayor, R. (1991). Testimony, action research, and empowerment: Puerto Rican women and popular education. In S. Gluck & D. Patai (Eds.), *Women's words.* New York: Routledge.

Benmayor, R., Torruellas, R. M., & Juarbe, A. (1992). *Responses to poverty among Puerto Rican women: Identity, community, and cultural citizenship.* New York: Centro de Estudios Puertorriquenos, City University of New York.

Berkowitz, B. (2001). *Prospecting among the poor: Welfare privatization.* Oakland, Calif.: Applied Research Center.

Berryman, P. (1987). *Liberation theology.* Philadelphia: Temple University Press.

Bickerton, R. (2006, March 6). What is the purpose of AELS? Posting on National Literacy Advocacy List, *aaace-nla@lists.literacytent.org.*

Bingman, M. B., Ebert, O., & Smith, M. (1999). *Changes in learners' lives one year after enrollment in literacy programs: An analysis from the longitudinal study of adult literacy participants in Tennessee.* Cambridge, Mass.: National Center for the Study of Adult Learning and Literacy, Harvard University.

Bloch, M. (2003). Global/Local analyses of the construction of family-child welfare. In M. Bloch, et al. (Eds.), *Governing children, families, and education: Restructuring the welfare state.* New York: Palgrave MacMillan.

Bloch, M., Holmlund, K., Moqvist, I., & Popkewitz, T. (Eds.). (2003). *Governing children, families, and education: Restructuring the welfare state.* New York: Palgrave MacMillan.

Boston Housing Authority. (2006). Annual Fiscal Plan for 2006. Retrieved June 29, 2006, from http://www.hud.gov/offices/pih/pha/approved/view_approved_plans.cfmma002v03.pdf.

Bourdieu, P. (1977). *Outline of theory and practice.* London: Cambridge University Press.

Bourdieu, P., & Passeron, J. C. (1977). *Reproduction in education, society, and culture.* London: Sage Publications.

Bowles, S., & Gintis, H. (1976). *Schooling in capitalist America.* New York: Basic Books.

Brady, J. (1994). Critical literacy, feminism, and a politics of representation. In P. McLaren & C. Lankshear (Eds.), *Politics of liberation: Paths from Freire.* New York: Routledge.

Brandwein, R. A. (1999). *Battered women, children, and welfare reform.* Thousand Oaks, Calif.: Sage Publications.

Bratt, R. (2000, March 12). The housing drought no one is talking about. *Boston Globe.*

Bratt, R., & Keyes, L. (1997). *New perspectives on self-sufficiency: Strategies of nonprofit housing organizations.* Medford, Mass.: Department of Urban and Environmental Policy, Tufts University.

Bratt, R., Stone, M., & Hartman, C. (2006). *A Right to housing: Foundation for a new social agenda.* Philadelphia: Temple University Press.

Braun, H., Jenkins, F., & Grigg, W. (2006). *Comparing private and public schools using hierarchical linear modeling.* (NCES 2006–461). Washington, D.C.: U.S. Department of Education, National Center for Education Statistics, Institute of Educational Sciences. Retrieved January 15, 2007, from: http://nces.ed.gov/nationsreportcard//pdf/studies/2006461.pdf.

Brodkey, L. (1991). Tropics of literacy. In C. Mitchell & K. Weiler (Eds.), *Rewriting literacy: Culture and the discourse of the other.* Westport, Conn.: Bergin & Garvey.

Brookfield, S. (1984). The contribution of Eduard Lindeman to the development of theory and philosophy in adult education. *Adult Education Quarterly, 34,* (4), 185–96.

Bunch, C., & Pollack, S. (Eds.) (1983). *Learning our way: Essays in feminist education.* New York: The Crossing Press.

Burg, M. A. (1994). Health problems of sheltered homeless women and their dependent children. *Health & Social Work, 19,* (2), 125–31.

Burge, K. (2006, January 24). Hub sees 9% rise in homelessness. *Boston Globe.*

Bushnell, D. (2006, August 3). As with state, local jobs on upswing. *Boston Globe.*

Cahill, S. (1999). *Tip of the iceberg or bump in the road? The initial impact of welfare reform in Dorchester.* Boston: Massachusetts Human Services Coalition.

Cain, A. J. (2003). Is the GED valuable to those who pass it? *Focus on Policy, 1,* (1), 1–5. Cambridge, Mass.: National Center for the Study of Adult Literacy & Learning, Harvard University.

Campolo, L. (1995). Developing educational self-esteem. *Connections: A Journal of Adult Literacy, 5,* 35–41.

Carmack, N. A. (1992). Women and illiteracy: The need for gender specific programming in literacy education. *Adult Basic Education, 2,* (3), 176–94.

Carnevale, A. P. (1999). *Education = success: Empowering Hispanic youth and adults.* Princeton, N.J.: Educational Testing Service.

Carnevale, A. P., & Desrochers, D. M. (1998). *Getting down to business: Matching welfare recipients' skills to jobs that train.* Princeton, N.J.: Educational Testing Service.

Carspecken, P. F. (1996). *Critical ethnography in educational research.* New York: Routledge.

Castells, M. (2000). *Vol. 1. The rise of the network society* (2nd ed.). Oxford: Blackwell Publishers.

Center for Budget and Policy Priorities (2006, June 28). CBPP statement on the New TANF regulations issued today by the Department of Health and Human Services. Retrieved July 5, 2006, from http://www.cbpp.org/6-28-06tanf-stmt.pdf.

Center for the Future of Children. (1997). Welfare to work, Special Issue. *The Future of Children, 7,* (1).

Center for Popular Education and Participatory Research. (2001). What is popular education? *Voices, 1,* (1), 1.

Center for Women Policy Studies. (2001). *Clipping our wings: The impact of welfare reform on the college aspirations of low-income women.* Washington, D.C.

Center for Women Policy Studies. (2002). *From poverty to self-sufficiency: The role of postsecondary education in welfare reform.* Washington, D.C.: Author.

Cervero, R., & Fitzpatrick, T. (1990). The enduring effects of family role and schooling on participation in adult education. *American Journal of Education, 99,* (1), 77–94.

City of Boston (2002). *Homelessness in the city of Boston, winter 2002-2003, annual census report.* Boston: Emergency Shelter Commission, City of Boston.

City of Boston (2005). *Homelessness in the city of Boston, winter 2005-2006, annual census report.* Boston: Emergency Shelter Commission, City of Boston.

Chacon, R. (1997, December 8). Study calls for overhaul of adult education: Mass jobs reported at stake. *Boston Globe,* p. A1.

Chaplin, D. (1999). *GED's for teenagers: Are there unintended consequences?* Washington, D.C.: Urban Institute.

Clifford, J., & Marcus, G. (Eds.). (1986). *Writing culture: The poetics and politics of ethnography.* Berkeley: University of California Press.

Clinton, B. (2006). How we ended welfare, together. *New York Times.* Retrieved August 22, 2006, from http://www.nytimes.com/2006/08/22/opinion/22clinton.html.

Clover, D. E., Follen, S., & Hall, B. (1998). *The nature of transformation: Environmental, adult, and popular education.* Toronto: University of Toronto Press.

Colclough, G., & Beck, E. M. (1986). The American educational structure and the reproduction of social class. *Sociological Inquiry, 56,* (4), 456–76.

Coley, R. J. (2001). *Differences in the gender gap: Comparisons across racial/ethnic groups in education and work.* Princeton, N.J.: Educational Testing Service.

Collins, D. (1977). *Paulo Freire: His life, works, and thought.* New York: Paulist Press.

Comings, J., Sum, A., & Uvin, J. (2000). *New skills for a new economy: Adult education's key role in sustaining economic growth and expanding opportunity.* Boston: Massachusetts Institute for a New Commonwealth (Mass INC).

Comings, J., Parrella, A., & Soricone, L. (1999). *Persistence among adult basic education students in pre-GED classes.* (NCSALL Report #12). Cambridge, Mass.: National Center for the Study of Adult Learning and Literacy, Harvard University.

Commonwealth of Massachusetts Department of Employment & Training. (1995). *The Massachusetts job outlook: An overview of job trends by industry.* Boston: Author.

Commonwealth of Massachusetts Department of Transitional Assistance. (1999). *How are they doing?: A longitudinal study of households leaving welfare under Massachusetts welfare reform.* Boston: Author.

Commonwealth of Massachusetts Department of Transitional Assistance. (1995). *Massachusetts welfare reform.* Boston: Author.

Commonwealth of Massachusetts Department of Education. (1999). An introduction to the National Reporting System. ABE Directors' Meeting, Leominster, Mass., October 27, 1999. Malden, Mass.: Author.

Commonwealth of Massachusetts Department of Education. (1999). Workforce Investment Act Basics 101: Serving students through inter-agency collaborations. ABE Directors' Meeting, Leominster, Mass., October 27, 1999. Malden, Mass.: Author.

Commonwealth of Massachusetts Department of Housing and Community Development. (2006). Streamlined annual plan for fiscal year 2006, April 14, 2006.

Retrieved June 26 2006, from http://www.mass.gov/dhcd/Temp/06/PHAplan/FinalPHAplan.pdf.

Corley, M. A. (2003). Poverty, racism, and literacy. *ERIC Digest, 243.* (Report No. EDO-CE-02-243).

Crandall, S., & Jain, S. (2005). *New directions in workforce development: Achieving success in the new economy: Which jobs help women reach economic self-sufficiency in Massachusetts?* Boston: The Women's Educational Industrial Union.

Creighton, S., & Hudson, L. (2002). *Participation trends and patterns in adult education: 1991–1999.* (NCES 2002-119) Washington, D.C.: National Center for Education Statistics, United States Department of Education.

Crowley, S. (2005, February 4). *Point of view, memo to members 10.5.* Washington, D.C.: National Low-Income Housing Coalition.

Council for Advancement of Adult Literacy (CAAL). (2002). *Research on research mini-survey.* New York: Author.

Dail, P. W. (1990). The psychosocial context of homeless mothers with young children. *Child Welfare, 69,* (4), 291–307.

D'Amico, D. (1996). The emperor's new jobs: Welfare reform, unemployment and education policy. *Urban Anthropology, 25,* (2), 165–94.

D'Amico, D. (1997). *Adult education and welfare to work initiatives: A review of research, practice, and policy.* Washington, D.C.: National Institute for Literacy.

D'Amico, D. (1998). *Writing poverty: Politics, policy, practice and personal responsibility adult education in the era of welfare reform.* Unpublished paper presented at the National Center for the Study of Adult Learning and Literacy conference, Rutgers University, July 19–21, 1998.

D'Amico, D. (2004). Race, class, gender, and sexual orientation in adult literacy: Power, pedagogy, and programs. In J. Comings, B. Garner, & C. Smith (Eds.), *Review of Adult Learning and Literacy, Volume 4.* Mahwah, N.J.: Lawrence Erlbaum.

Degener, S. C. (2001). Making sense of critical pedagogy in adult literacy education. In J. Comings, B. Garner, & C. Smith (Eds.), *Annual Review of Adult Learning and Literacy, Volume 2.* San Francisco: Jossey-Bass.

Dei-Sefa, G. J., Mazzuca, J., McIsaac, E., and Zine, J. (1997). *Reconstructing "drop-out": A critical ethnography of the dynamics of black students' disengagement from school.* Toronto: University of Toronto Press.

Delgado-Gaitan, C. (1990). *Literacy for empowerment: The role of parents in children's education.* Bristol, Pa.: Falmer Press.

Demetrion, G. (2005). *Conflicting paradigms in adult literacy education: In quest of a U.S. democratic politics of literacy.* Mahwah, N.J.: Lawrence Erlbaum.

DeParle, J. (1999, November 28). "Early sex abuse hinders many women on welfare." *New York Times.*

DeSanctis, V. (1979). *The Adult Education Act, 1964–1979: A political history.* Upper Montclair, N.J.: National Adult Education Clearinghouse, Montclair State College. (ERIC Document Reproduction Service No. ED 218 517).

Devine, J. (1994). "Literacy and social power." In B. M. Ferdman, R. Weber, & A. G. Ramirez (Eds.), *Literacy across languages & cultures.* Albany: State University of New York Press.

Dodson, L. (1999). *Don't call us out of name.* Boston: Beacon Press.
Dolby, N., Dimitriadis, G., & Willis, P. (Eds.) (2004). *Learning to labor in new times.* New York: Routledge.
Dorn, S. (2003). High-stakes testing and the history of graduation. *Education Policy Analysis Archives, 11,* (1), 1–29.
Dowdy, J. (2003). *GED stories: Black women and their struggle for social equity.* New York: Peter Lang Publishers.
Dudley Street Neighborhood Initiative (DSNI). (1996). *Urban village vision process: Towards a wholesome community.* Boston: Urban Village Working Group, Dudley Street Neighborhood Initiative.
Dudley Street Neighborhood Initiative (DSNI). (2003). *Dudley neighborhood profile.* Boston: Urban Village Working Group, Dudley Street Neighborhood Initiative.
Dujon, D., & Withorn, A. (Eds.). (1996). *For crying out loud: Women's poverty in the United States.* Boston: South End Press.
Edin, K., & Lein, L. (1997). *Making ends meet: How single mothers survive welfare and low-wage work.* New York: Russell Sage Foundation.
Ellis, J. (1984). *A history and analysis of the Adult Education Act, 1964–1984.* (ERIC Document Reproduction Service No. ED 252 658).
Ellison, A. (2007, January 10). ABE Wait Lists. Message posted to National Literacy Advocacy List, http://aaace-nla-bounces@lists.literacytent.org.
Emrath, P. (2005). NAHB study finds housing options particularly limited for retail sales workers. Retrieved July 23, 2005, from http://www.nahb.org/fileUpload_details.aspx?contentID=42013.
Fass, S., & Garner, B. (2000). *Beyond the GED: Making conscious choices about the GED and your future.* Cambridge, Mass.: National Center for the Study of Adult Literacy & Learning, Harvard University.
Ferreira, E. C., & Ferreira, J. C. (1997). *Making sense of the media: A handbook of popular education techniques.* New York: Monthly Review Press.
Fetterman, D. M. (1989). *Ethnography: Step by step. Applied social research methods, Volume 17.* Newbury Park, Calif.: Sage Publications.
Fine, M. (1991). *Framing dropouts: Notes on the politics of an urban public high school.* Albany: State University of New York Press.
Fine, M., & Zane, N. (1991). Bein' wrapped too tight: When low-income women drop out of high school. *Women's Studies Quarterly, 19,* 77–99.
Finegold, K., Wherry, L., & Schardin, S. (2004). *Block grants: Details of the Bush proposals.* Washington, D.C.: Urban Institute.
Finegold, K., Wherry, L., & Schardin, S. (2004). *Block grants: Historical overview and lessons learned.* Washington, D.C.: Urban Institute.
Fingeret, H. A. (1983). Social network: A new perspective on independence and illiterate adults. *Adult Education Quarterly, 33,* (3), 133–46.
Fingeret, H. A. (1990). Changing literacy instruction: Moving beyond the status quo. In F. P. Chisman (Ed.), *Leadership for literacy: The agenda for the 1990s.* San Francisco: Jossey Bass.
Fingeret, H. A., & Drennon, C. (1997). *Literacy for life: Adult learners, new practices.* New York: Teachers College Press.
Foley, G. (1998). Clearing the theoretical ground: Elements in a theory of popular education. *International Review of Education, 44,* (2–3), 139–58.

Foucault, M. (1980). *Power/knowledge: Selected interviews and other writings, 1972–1977.* New York: Pantheon Books.

Fraser, N., & Gordon, L. (1994). A genealogy of dependency: Tracing a keyword of the U.S. welfare state. *Signs: Journal of Women in Culture and Society, 19,* (2), 309–36.

Freeman, R. (1993). How much has de-unionization contributed to the rise in male earnings inequality? In S. Danziger & P. Gottschalk (Eds.), *Uneven tides: Rising inequality in America.* New York: Russell Sage Foundation.

Freire, P. (1973). *Education for critical consciousness.* New York: Seabury Press.

Freire, P. (1985). *The politics of education: Culture, power, and liberation.* Westport, Conn.: Bergin & Garvey.

Freire, P. (1990). *Pedagogy of the oppressed.* New York: Continuum.

Freire, P., & Macedo, D. (1987). *Literacy: Reading the word and the world.* Westport, Conn.: Bergin & Garvey.

Gadotti, M. (1994). *Reading Paulo Freire: His life and work.* Albany: State University of New York Press.

Gailbraith, M. W. (1990). Education through community organizations. In *New Directions for Adult and Continuing Education.* San Francisco: Jossey-Bass.

Gavin, R. (2006, July 21). June ends "jobs deficit" for Romney. *Boston Globe.*

Gee, J. P. (1986). Orality and literacy: From the savage mind to ways with words. *TESOL Quarterly, 20,* 719–46.

Gee, J. P. (1989). Orality and literacy: From "savage mind" to "ways with words". *Journal of Education, 1,* 39–60.

Giroux, H. (1981). *Ideology, culture, and the process of schooling.* Philadelphia: Temple University Press.

Giroux, H. (1983). *Theory and resistance in education: A pedagogy for the opposition.* Westport, Conn.: Bergin & Garvey.

Giroux, H. (1988a). *Schooling and the struggle for public life: Critical pedagogy in the modern age.* Minneapolis: University of Minneapolis Press.

Giroux, H. (1988b). *Teachers as intellectuals: Toward a critical pedagogy of learning.* Westport, Conn.: Bergin & Garvey.

Giroux, H. (1989). Schooling as a form of cultural politics: Toward a pedagogy of and for difference. In H. Giroux & P. McLaren (Eds.), *Critical pedagogy, the state, and cultural struggle.* Albany: State University of New York Press.

Giroux, H. (1994). *Between borders: Pedagogy and the politics of cultural studies.* New York: Routledge.

Giroux, H. (2004). Neoliberalism and the demise of democracy: Resurrecting hope in dark times [Electronic version]. *Dissent Voice.* Retrieved July 25, 2005, from http://www.dissidentvoice.org/Aug04/Giroux0807.htm.

Goffman, E. (1986). *Stigma: Notes on the management of spoiled identity.* New York: Touchstone Books.

Goodman, L., Saxe, L., & Harvey, M. (1991). Homelessness as psychological trauma. *American Psychologist, 46,* (11), 1219–25.

Gordon, L. (Ed.). (1990). *Women, the state, and welfare.* Madison: University of Wisconsin Press.

Gramsci, A. (1971). *Selections from the prison notebooks.* Q. Hoare & N. Smith (Eds.). New York: International Publishers.

Graves, B. (1979). What is liberatory education? A conversation with Myles Horton. *Radical Teacher, 12,* 3–5.
Greenberg, D. (2002). Case statement. In G. Spangenberg, (Ed.), *Making the case: Adult education and literacy, key to America's future.* New York: Council for Advancement of Adult Literacy.
Greenberg, D. (2003). Women and Literacy. Retrieved February 19, 2003, from http://www.litwomen.org/Research/Greenberg.html.
Greenberg, M., & Parrott, S. (2006). *Summary of TANF work participation provisions in the Budget Reconciliation Bill.* Washington, D.C.: Center for Budget and Policy Priorities and Center for Law and Social Policy. Retrieved June 26, 2006, from: http://www.cbpp.org/1-18-06tanf.htm.
Gross, T. (1997). Introduction. In E. Ferreira & J. S. Ferreira (Eds.), *Making sense of the media: A handbook of popular education techniques.* New York: Monthly Review Press.
Guerra, J. C. (1991). The role of ethnography in the reconceptualization of literacy. *Quarterly Newsletter of the Laboratory of Comparative Human Cognition, 13,* (1), 3–9.
Gustafson, K. (2005). *To punish the poor: Criminalizing trends in the welfare system.* Oakland, Calif.: Women of Color Resource Center.
Haig-Friedman, D. (2000). *Parenting in public: Family shelter and public assistance.* New York: Columbia University.
Hallgren, C., & Weiner, G. (2003). The web, anti-racism, education and the state in Sweden: Why here? Why now? In M. Bloch, et al. (Eds.), *Governing children, families, and education.* New York: Palgrave MacMillan.
Hamal-Gurung, S., & Rivera, L. (2003). *Multiple identities and shifting boundaries: Insider research in marginalized communities.* Paper presented at the 53rd Annual Meeting of the Society for the Study of Social Problems, Atlanta.
Hamilton, G. (2002). *Moving people from welfare to work: Lessons from the national evaluation of welfare-to-work strategies.* Retrieved October 19, 2005, from http://www.mdrc.org/publications/52/summary.html.
Haney, W. (2004). *The education pipeline in the United States, 1970–2000.* Boston: National Board on Educational Testing and Public Policy, Boston College.
Harrison, B., & Bluestone, B. (1988). *The great U-turn.* New York: Basic Books.
Hart, M. (1995). Motherwork: A radical proposal to rethink work and education. In M. Welton (Ed.), *In defense of the lifeworld: Critical perspectives on adult learning.* Albany: State University of New York Press.
Hayes, E. (1999). Policy issues that drive the transformation of adult literacy. In *The welfare to work challenge for adult literacy educators. New Directions for Adult and Continuing Education.* San Francisco: Jossey-Bass.
Hayes, E. (1992). *Toward new perspectives on women in adult education.* Paper presented at the Adult Education Research Conference, Saskatchewan, Canada, May 15–17, 1992. (ERIC Document Reproduction Service No. ED368 856).
Hayes, E. (2000). Youth in adult literacy education programs. In J. Comings, B. Garner, and C. Smith (Eds.), *Annual Review of Adult Learning and Literacy, Volume 1.* San Francisco: Jossey-Bass.
Hayes, E., & Flannery, D. (2000). *Women as learners: The significance of gender in adult learning.* San Francisco: Jossey-Bass.
Hayes, E., & Smith, L. (1994). Women in adult education: An analysis of perspectives in major journals. *Adult Education Quarterly, 44,* (4), 201–21.

Hays, S. (2003). *Flat broke with children: Women in the age of welfare reform.* New York: Oxford University Press.

Haywoode, T. (1991). *Working-class feminism: Creating a politics of community connection and concern.* Doctoral dissertation. Graduate Center, City University of New York.

Heaney, T. (1996). *Adult education for social change: From center stage to the wings and back again.* (Report No. 365). Columbus: Center on Education and Training for Employment, Ohio State University. (ERIC Document Reproduction Service No. ED 396 190).

Herbert, B. (2005, July 21). Education's collateral damage. *New York Times.*

Herbert, B. (2006, July 3). Working for a pittance. *New York Times.*

Holton, W. (1997). *HOPE: 50 years of the Little Sisters of the Assumption on Magnolia Street in Dorchester.* Unpublished paper. Boston: Department of Sociology, Northeastern University.

hooks, b. (1984). *Feminist theory: From margin to center.* Boston: South End Press.

hooks, b. (1989). *Talking back: Thinking feminist/ Thinking black.* Boston: South End Press.

hooks, b. (1994). *Teaching to transgress: Education as the practice of freedom.* New York: Routledge.

Holzer, H. (1996). *What employers want: Job prospects for less educated workers.* New York: Russell Sage Foundation.

Horsman, J. (2000). *Too scared to learn: Women, violence, and education.* Mahwah, N.J.: Lawrence Erlbaum.

Horton, A. I. (1989). *The Highlander Folk School: A history of its major programs, 1932–1961.* New York: Carlson Publishing.

Horton, M., & Freire, P. (1990). *We make the road by walking: Conversations on education and social change.* Philadelphia: Temple University Press.

Howe, P. (1994, November 26). Welfare deal faces tough sell in House committee, head dismisses compromise negotiations. *Boston Globe,* Metro p. 17.

Howe, P. (1994, November 29). Weld, 2 senators forge welfare deal. *Boston Globe,* Metro pp. 33–36.

Hull, G. (1997). Hearing other voices: A critical assessment of popular views on literacy and work. In G. Hull (Ed.), *Changing work, changing workers: Critical perspectives on language, literacy, and skills.* Albany: State University of New York Press.

Hunter, C., & Harman, D. (1979). *Adult illiteracy in the United States: A report to the Ford Foundation.* New York: McGraw Hill.

Imel, S. (2000). Welfare to work: Considerations for adult and vocational education programs. *ERIC Digest,* 216.

Jacobs, L. (2005). Legal momentum. Congressional testimony before House on Ways and Means, Subcommittee on Human Resources. February 10, 2005.

Jencks, C. (1994). *The homeless.* Cambridge, Mass.: Harvard University Press.

Jurmo, P. (1989). The case for participatory literacy education. In H. A. Fingeret & P. Jurmo (Eds.), *Participatory literacy education.* San Francisco: Jossey-Bass.

Kahn, P., & Polakow, V. (2000). *Struggling to stay in school: Obstacles to postsecondary education under the welfare-to-work regime in Michigan.* Ann Arbor: Center for the Education of Women, University of Michigan.

Kates, E. (2004). Debunking the myth of the failure of education and training. In V. Polakow, et al. (Eds.), *Shut out: Low-income mothers and higher education in post-welfare America.* Albany: State University of New York Press.

Kates, E. (1999). Public assistance and workforce development: The growing divide. In *Connection: New England's Journal of Higher Education and Economic Development, 14,* (1), 52–54.

Katz, M. B. (1995). *Improving poor people: The welfare state, the underclass, and urban schools as history.* Ewing, N.J.: Princeton University Press.

Kim, K., Collins-Hagedorn, M., Williamson, J., & Chapman, C. (2004). *Participation in adult education and lifelong learning: 2000–2001 (NCES 2004-050).* Washington, D.C.: National Center for Education Statistics, United States Department of Education.

Knell, S. (1997). *Learn to earn: Issues raised by welfare reform for adult education, training and work.* Washington, D.C.: National Institute for Literacy.

Kozol, J. (1991). *Savage inequalities: Children in America's schools.* New York: Crown Publishers.

Kurtz, M. (2003, August 14). Tests seen increasing dropout rates. *Boston Globe.*

Lankshear, C., & McLaren, P. (Eds.). (1993). *Critical literacy: Politics, praxis, and the postmodern.* Albany: State University of New York Press.

Leonard, M. A. (1999). *We need to stand together: The impact of welfare reform on the Dudley street neighborhood and the community's response to the challenge.* Boston: Dudley Street Neighborhood Initiative.

Levenson, A., Reardon, E., & Schmidt, S. R. (1998). *The employment prospects of welfare recipients in the most populous U.S. counties: Limited skills mean limited employment opportunities.* Unpublished paper presented at the National Center for the Study of Adult Learning and Literacy conference, Rutgers University, July 19–21, 1998.

Levine, H., and L. Harmon (1992). *The death of an American Jewish community.* New York: The Free Press.

Levy, F. (1987). *Dollars and dreams: The changing American income distribution.* New York: Russell Sage Foundation.

Lewin, T., & Medina, J. (2003, August 31). To cut failure rate, schools shed students. *New York Times.*

Liebow, E. (1993). *Tell them who I am: The lives of homeless women.* New York: The Free Press.

Livingstone, D. W. (Ed.). (1987). *Critical pedagogy and cultural power.* Westport, Conn.: Bergin & Garvey.

Lofland, J., & Lofland, L. (1995). *Analyzing Social Settings, 3rd Edition.* Belmont, Calif.: Wadsworth Publishers.

Loprest, P. (1999). *Families who left welfare: Who are they and how are they doing.* Washington, D.C.: The Urban Institute.

Luke, C., & Gore, J. (Eds.). (1992). *Feminisms & critical pedagogy.* New York: Routledge.

Luttrell, W. (1993). The teachers, they all had their pets: Concepts of gender, knowledge, and power. *Signs: Journal of women in culture and society, 18,* (3), 505–47.

Luttrell, W. (1997). *Schoolsmart and motherwise: Working-class women's identity and schooling.* New York: Routledge.

Luttrell, W. (2003). *Pregnant bodies, fertile minds: Gender, race, and the schooling of pregnant teens.* New York: Routledge.
Lyon-Callo, V. (2004). *Inequality, poverty, and neoliberal governance: An activist ethnography in the homeless sheltering industry.* Orchard Park, N.Y.: Broadview Press.
Macedo, D. (1991). The politics of emancipatory literacy in Cape Verde. In C. Mitchell & K. Weiler (Eds.). *Rewriting literacy: Culture and the discourse of the other.* Westport, Conn.: Bergin & Garvey.
Macedo, D. (1994). *Literacies of power: What Americans are not allowed to know.* Boulder, Colo.: Westview Press.
Martin, R. (2001). *Listening up: Reinventing ourselves as teachers and students.* Portsmouth, N.H.: Boynton/Cook Publishers.
Marx, K. (1964). *The economic and philosophic manuscripts of 1844.* New York International Publishers.
Marx, K. (1972). *The German ideology.* New York: International Publishers.
Marx, K. (1976). *Capital: Volume 1.* New York: Penguin Books.
Massachusetts Budget and Policy Center (2004). *The state of working Massachusetts 2004: Down but not out.* Retrieved August 6, 2006, from http://www.massbudget.org/article.php?id=253.
Massachusetts Budget and Policy Center (2006). *The growing gap: Income inequality in Massachusetts.* Retrieved August 5, 2006, from http://www.massbudget.org/article.php?id=385.
Massachusetts Coalition for the Homeless. (2006). Fact Sheets. Retrieved July 2, 2006, from http://www.mahomeless.org/facts/factsoverviewfamily.html.
McCorkel, J. (2004). Criminally dependent? Gender, punishment, and the rhetoric of welfare reform. *Social Politics: International Studies in Gender, State, & Society 11,* (3), 386–410.
McLaren, P. (1989b). On ideology and education: Critical pedagogy and the cultural politics of resistance. In H. A. Giroux & P. McLaren (Eds.), *Critical pedagogy, the state, and cultural struggle.* Albany: State University of New York Press.
McLaren, P. (1993). *Schooling as a ritual performance, 2nd ed.* New York: Routledge.
McLaren, P. (1994). Multiculturalism and the postmodern critique: Toward a pedagogy of resistance and transformation. In H. A. Giroux & P. McLaren (Eds.), *Between borders: pedagogy and the politics of cultural studies.* New York: Routledge.
McLaren, P. L. (1995). Critical pedagogy in the age of global capitalism: Some challenges for the educational left. *Australian Journal of Education, 39,* (1), 5–21.
McLaren, P. L. (1998). *Life in schools: An introduction to critical pedagogy in the foundations of education, 3rd Edition.* White Plains, N.Y.: Longman Press.
McLaren, P. L., & Giarelli, J. M. (Eds.). (1995). *Critical theory and educational research.* Albany: State University of New York Press.
McLaren, P., & Scatamburlo-D'Annibale,V. (2004). Paul Willis, class consciousness, and critical pedagogy: Toward a socialist future. In Dolby, et al. (Eds.), *Learning to labor in new times.* New York: Routledge.
McLaughlin, D., & Tierney, W. G. (1993). *Naming silenced lives: Personal narratives and the process of educational change.* New York: Routledge.
Mead, L. (2005). The reauthorization of TANF: Work and childcare provisions.

Congressional testimony, Committee on Education and the Workforce, U.S. House of Representatives, 109th Congress. March 15, 2005.

Mechum, T. (2004). New GED policies and the one-year rule. *Field Notes, 13*, (4), 3–4.

Medoff, P., & Sklar, H. (1993). *Streets of hope: The fall and rise of an urban neighborhood.* Boston: South End Press.

Merrow, J. (2004, November 30). Disappearing dropouts. PBS News Hour Radio Program. Retrieved December 1, 2005, from http://www.pbs.org/newshour/bb/education/july-dec04/dropouts_11-30.html.

Miller, M., & Alexander, I. (Eds.). Women and literacy: Moving to power and participation. *Women's Studies Quarterly, 32* (1/2).

Mitchell, C., & Weiler, K. (Eds.). (1991). *Rewriting literacy: Culture and the discourse of the other.* Westport, Conn.: Bergin & Garvey.

Moffitt, R. A. (2002). *From welfare to work: What the evidence shows. Policy brief no. 13.* Washington, D.C.: The Brookings Institution.

Moraga, C., & Anzaldua, G. (Eds.). (1983). *This bridge called my back: Writings by radical women of color.* New York: Kitchen Table Press.

Morrish, E., Horsman, J., & Hofer, J. (2002). *Take on the challenge: A sourcebook from the women, violence and adult education project.* Boston: World Education.

Moscovitch, E. (1997). *Closing the gap: Raising skills to raise wages.* Boston: Massachusetts Institute for a New Commonwealth.

Mouffe, C. (Ed.). (1979). *Gramsci and Marxist Theory.* Boston: Routledge & Kegan Paul.

Murnane, R., Willett, J., & Boudett, K. P. (1995). Do high school dropouts benefit from Obtaining a GED? *Educational Evaluation and Policy Analysis, 17*, (2), 133–47.

Murphy, G. (2003). *The nation's adult education and literacy system.* Washington, D.C.: National Coalition for Literacy, National Council of State Directors of Adult Education.

Na'im, A., & Wagman, N. (2005). *Kids, cuts, and consequences: How cuts to effective programs hurt our children.* Boston: Massachusetts Budget and Policy Center.

National Center for Education Statistics. (2000). *Participation in adult education in the United States: 1998–1999.* Washington, D.C.: National Center for Education Statistics, Office of Educational Research and Improvement, U.S. Department of Education.

National Council of State Directors of Adult Education. (2005). *Response to the OMB Program Assessment Rating Tool (PART).* Retrieved April 8, 2005, from http://www.ncsdae.org/myweb/State_Directors_Response.htm.

National Institute for Literacy. (1998). *Literacy it's a whole new world: Campaign kit materials.* Washington, D.C.: National Institute for Literacy.

National Institute for Literacy. (2000). *From the margins to the mainstream: An action agenda for literacy.* Washington, D.C.: National Literacy Summit 2000, National Institute for Literacy.

National Institute for Literacy. (2000). *National Literacy Summit 2000 foundation paper.* Washington, D.C.: Author.

National Law Center on Homelessness and Poverty. (2003). Summary of the

McKinney Homeless Assistance Act. Retrieved December 8, 2003, from http://www.serve.org/nche.

Newman, K. S. (1999). *No shame in my game: The working poor in the inner city.* New York: Vintage.

Nolan, K., & Anyon, J. (2004). Learning to do time: Willis's model of cultural reproduction in an era of postindustrialism, globalization, and mass incarceration. In N. Dolby, G. Dimitriadis, and P. Willis (Eds.), *Learning to labor in new times.* New York: Routledge Farmer.

Norris, J. A., & Kennington, P. (1992). *Developing literacy programs for homeless adults.* Malabar, Fl.: Krieger Publishing.

Olsen, M. (1996). In defence of the welfare state and publicly provided education: A New Zealand perspective. *Journal of Education Policy, 11,* (3), 337–62.

Pachikara, S. (1998). *Welfare reform and barriers to work in Massachusetts.* Boston: McCormack Institute, University of Massachusetts-Boston.

Parrott, S., & Sherman, A. (2006). *TANF at 10: Program results are more mixed than often understood.* Washington, D.C.: Center on Budget and Policy Priorities.

Passaro, J. (1996). *The unequal homeless: Men on the streets, women in their place.* New York: Routledge.

Pearce, D. (1978). The feminization of poverty. *Urban and Social Change Review, 11,* (1), 28–36.

Pearce, D., Russell, L. H., & Brooks, J. (1998). *The self-sufficiency standard for Massachusetts: Executive summary.* Washington, D.C.: Wider Opportunities for Women, Inc.

Pietri, P. (1973). *Puerto Rican obituary.* New York: Monthly Review Press.

Piven, F. F., & Cloward, R. (1971). *Regulating the poor: The functions of public welfare.* New York: Vintage.

Piven, F. F., & Cloward, R. (1977). *Poor people's movements: How they succeed and why they fail.* New Orleans: Pantheon.

Piven, F. F., & Cloward, R. (1982). *The new class war.* New York: Pantheon.

Polakow, V. (1993). *Lives on the edge: single mothers and their children in the other America.* Chicago: University of Chicago Press.

Polakow, V. (2003). *Summary of rights denied: Student mothers' stories of struggle and resistance under the welfare regime 1997–2002.* Paper presented at the American Education Research Association conference, April 21–25, 2003.

Polakow, V., Butler, S., Deprez, L., & Kahn, P. (2004). *Shut out: Low-income women and higher education in postwelfare America.* Albany: State University of New York Press.

Project Hope. (1984). *Mission statement.* Boston: Author.

Project South. (2002). *Today's globalization. 2nd edition.* Atlanta: Author.

ProLiteracy Worldwide (2003). *The number of functionally illiterate adults in U.S. is growing.* New York.

ProLiteracy Worldwide (2006). *The state of adult literacy 2006.* Syracuse, N.Y..

Purcell-Gates, V. (1995). *Other people's words: The cycle of low literacy.* Cambridge, Mass.: Harvard University Press.

Quigley, B. A. (1989). *Reasons for resistance to ABE and recommendations for new delivery models and instructional strategies for the future.* Monroeville: Continuing and Graduate Education Center, Pennsylvania State University.

Quigley, B. A. (1990). This immense evil: The history of literacy education as social policy. In T. Valentine (Ed.), *Beyond rhetoric: Fundamental issues in adult literacy education.* Athens: Department of Adult Education, University of Georgia.

Quigley, B. A. (1992). Looking back in anger: The influences of schooling on illiterate adults. *Journal of Education, 174,* (1), 104–21.

Quigley, B. A. (1997). *Rethinking literacy education: The critical need for practice-based change.* San Francisco: Jossey-Bass.

Reder, S. (1987). Comparative aspects of functional literacy development: Three ethnic communities. In D. Wagner (Ed.), *The future of literacy in a changing world.* Oxford: Pergamon Press.

Reder, S. (1990). *Literacy across languages & cultures.* Unpublished paper presented at Third Gutenberg Conference, Ithaca, N.Y. (ERIC Document Reproduction Service No. ED 318 279).

Reder S., & Strawn, C. (2001). The K-12 school experiences of high school dropouts. *Focus on Basics, 4,* (D), 1–5.

Reuys, S. (1997). Welfare's retreat from education: Exploring the impact of Massachusetts welfare reform on adult basic education. *All Write News.* Boston: Adult Literacy Resource Institute.

Reuys, S. (2002). ABE opposes funding cuts, survives state budget crisis. *All Write News, XVIII,* 4, 1–3. Boston: Adult Literacy Resource Institute.

Rifkin, J. (1995). *The end of work.* New York: G. P. Putnam.

Ripke, M. N., & Crosby, D. A. (2002). The effects of welfare reform on the educational outcomes of parents and their children. In W. Secada (Ed.), *Review of Research in Education, 26,* (1), 181–261.

Rivera, K. (1999a). Popular research and social transformation: A community-based approach to critical pedagogy. *TESOL Quarterly, 33,* (3), 485–500.

Rivera, K. (1999b). From developing one's voice to making oneself heard: Affecting language policy from the bottom up. In T. Huebner & K. Davis (Eds.), *Sociopolitical perspectives on language policy and planning in the USA.* Philadelphia: John Benjamins.

Rivera, L. (2001). Learning community: An ethnographic study of popular education and homeless women in a shelter-based adult literacy program (Doctoral dissertation, Northeastern University, 2001). *Dissertation Abstracts International, 61,* (09A), 3511.

Rivera, L. (2003). Changing women: An ethnographic study of homeless mothers and popular education. *Journal of Sociology and Social Welfare, 30,* (2), 31–51.

Rivera, L. (2004a). Learning community: Popular education and homeless women. *Women's Studies Quarterly, 32,* (1–2), 196–212.

Rivera, L. (2004b). Literacy for change: Latina adult learners and popular education. In R. Ybarra & N. Lopez (Eds.), *Creating alternative discourses in the education of Latinos & Latinas: A reader.* New York: Peter Lang Publishers.

Rivera, L. (2005). Social inequality, education, and social mobility. *Democracy & Education, 15,* (2), 34–38.

Rockhill, K. (1990). Literacy as threat/desire: Longing to be somebody. *TESL Talk, 20,* (1), 89–110.

Rockhill, K. (1993). (Dis)connecting literacy and sexuality: Speaking the unspeakable in the classroom. In C. Lankshear & P. McLaren (Eds.), *Critical literacy: Politics, praxis, and the postmodern.* Albany: State University of New York Press.

Roofless Women's Action Research Mobilization. (1997). *Lifting the voices of homeless women: Summary of findings and recommendations.* Boston: Center for Community Planning, University of Massachusetts-Boston.

Rose, A. D. (1991). *Ends or means: An overview of the history of the Adult Education Act.* Columbus: Center on Education and Training for Employment, Ohio State University. (ERIC Document Reproduction Service No. ED 341 875).

Rose, N. (1999). *Powers of freedom: Reframing political thought.* London: Cambridge University Press.

Ryan, W. (1999, January). The new landscape for nonprofits. *Harvard Business Review,* 1–10.

Sard, B., & Springer, J. (2002). Affordable housing: One of the keys to self-sufficiency. *Housing Facts & Findings, 4,* (1), 1–7.

Schemo, D. J. (2006, July 15). Public schools perform near private ones in study. *New York Times.*

Schillinger, E. (1988). Dependency, control, and isolation: Battered women and the welfare system. *Journal of Contemporary Ethnography, 16,* (4), 469–90.

Schnapp, S. (1998). *Introduction to popular education* [Course lectures]. Medford, Mass.: Lincoln Filene Center, Tufts University.

Schram, S. F. (2000). *After welfare: The culture of postindustrial social policy.* New York: New York University Press.

Schugurensky, D. (1998). The legacy of Paulo Freire: A critical review of his contributions. *Convergence, 31,* (1/2), 17–29.

Schwartzman, H. B. (1993). *Ethnography in organizations. Qualitative research methods. Volume 27.* Newbury Park, Calif.: Sage Publishers.

Sennott, C. (1994, February 20). Finding 4 generations sustained by welfare family of abuse suspect has dozens on public aid. *Boston Globe,* Metro, pp.1–8.

Sennott, C., & Armstrong, D. (1994, April 12). Kin feel abuse suspect has fled, Ventura called from Puerto Rico. *Boston Globe,* Metro, pp. 25–27.

Shaw, K. M., Goldrick-Rab, S., Mazzeo, C., & Jacobs, J. (2006). *Putting poor people to work: How the work-first idea eroded college access for the poor.* New York: Russell Sage Foundation.

Shook, M., & Peterson, J. (Eds.). (1991). *Streets are for nobody: Homeless women speak.* Boston: Boston Center for the Arts.

Shor, I. (1992). *Empowering education.* Chicago: University of Chicago Press.

Shor, I., & Freire, P. (1987). *A pedagogy for liberation.* Westport, Conn.: Bergin & Garvey.

Simon, R. I. (1992). *Teaching against the grain: Texts for a pedagogy of possibility.* Westport, Conn.: Bergin & Garvey.

Simon, R. I., & Dippo, D. (1986). On critical ethnographic work. *Anthropology & Education Quarterly, 17,* 195–202.

Sleeter, C. E., & McLaren, P. (Eds.). (1995). *Multicultural education, critical pedagogy, and the politics of difference.* Albany: State University of New York Press.

Smith, B. (Ed.). (1983). *Home girls: A black feminist anthology.* New York: Kitchen Table Press.

Smythe, S., & Isserlis, J. (2003). The good mother: Exploring mothering discourses in family literacy texts. *Family Literacy Forum, 2,* (2), 25–33.

Snow, C. E., Barnes, W. S., Chandler, J., Goodman, I. F., & Hemphill, L. (1991). *Unfulfilled expectations: Home and school influences on literacy.* Cambridge, Mass.: Harvard University Press.

Spangenberg, G. (Ed.). (2002). *Making the case: Adult education & literacy, key to America's future.* New York: Council for Advancement of Adult Literacy.

Spangenberg, G. (2004, June 30). Who's accountable in the drop in HS/GEDs in AELS? Message posted to http://lists.literacytent.org.

Spanos, G. (1991). *Cultural considerations in adult literacy education.* Washington, D.C.: National Clearinghouse on Literacy Education. (ERIC Document Reproduction Service No. ED 334 866).

Sparks, B. (1998). The politics of culture and the struggle to get an education. *Adult Education Quarterly, 48,* (4), 245–59.

Sparks, B. (1999). Critical issues and dilemmas for adult literacy programs. *The welfare to work challenge for adult literacy educators. New Directions for Adult and Continuing Education.* San Francisco: Jossey-Bass.

Sparks, B. (2003). Challenges welfare mothers face as educational advocates implement welfare policy. Paper presented at the American Education Research Association conference, April 21–25, 2003, Chicago.

Speights, D. (2001). The year 1999 in review. *Annual Review of Adult Learning and Literacy, Volume 2.* San Francisco: Jossey Bass.

Sperazi, L., Connelly, M., Knudsen, A., Turtle, M., Fried, M., & Oberfield, A. (1990). *Finding myself; finding my home: An evaluation of the Adult Education with Homeless Persons Project for the Massachusetts Department of Education.* Wellesley, Mass.: The Stone Center, Wellesley College. (ERIC Document Reproduction Service No. ED 350 424).

Stack, C. (1974). *All our kin.* New York: Basic Books.

Stein, S. (2000). *Equipped for the future: A customer-driven vision for adult literacy and lifelong learning.* Washington, D.C.: National Institute for Literacy.

Steinberg, A., Johnson, C., & Pennington, H. (2006). *Addressing America's dropout challenge: State efforts to boost graduation rates require federal support.* Boston: Jobs for the Future.

Stewart, D. W., & Shamdasani, P. N. (1990). *Focus groups: Theory and practice.* Newbury Park, Calif.: Sage Publishers.

Sticht, T. (1998). *Moving adult literacy education from the margins of educational policy and practice.* Washington, D.C.: Office of Vocational and Adult Education, U.S. Department of Education.

Sticht, T. (2002). The rise of the adult education and literacy system in the United States 1600–2000. In J. Comings, B. Garner, & C. Smith (Eds.), *Annual Review of Adult Learning and Literacy: Volume 3.* San Francisco: Jossey-Bass.

Sticht, T. (2005, July 16). Moving the adult education and literacy system from the margins to the mainstream of education in the U.S.: Grounds for new hope. Message posted to http://aaace-nla@lists.literacytent.org.

Stoll, M. A., Melendez, E., and Montrichard, A. (2003). *Will community-based employment and training organizations be disadvantaged under WIA? Recent evidence on participant characteristics and outcomes in Boston.* Los Angeles: Center for the Study of Urban Poverty, University of California Los Angeles.

Stone, M. E. (1993). *Shelter poverty: New ideas on housing affordability.* Philadelphia: Temple University Press.

Street, B. V. (1984). *Literacy in theory and practice.* London: Cambridge University Press.

Sum, A., Kirsch, I., & Yamamoto, K. (2004). *Pathways to labor market success: The literacy proficiency of U.S. adults.* Princeton, N.J.: Educational Testing Services.

Susser, I. (1988). Working-class women, social protest, and changing ideologies. In A. Bookman & S. Morgen (Eds.), *Women and the politics of empowerment.* Philadelphia: Temple University Press.

Takaki, R. (1993). *A different mirror: A history of multicultural America.* New York: Back Bay Books.

Taylor, D., & Dorsey-Gaines, C. (1988). *Growing up literate: Learning from inner city families.* Portsmouth, N.H.: Heinemann Publishers.

Thacker, J. (2002, September 4). Education free for all. *Boston's Weekly Dig.*

Thomas, J. (1993). *Doing critical ethnography: Qualitative research methods, Volume 26.* Newbury Park, Calif.: Sage Publishers.

Thompson, J. (1980). Adult education and the disadvantaged. In J. Thompson (Ed.), *Adult education for a change.* London: Hutchinson.

Thornburgh, N. (2006, April 11). Does a GED really do the Job?: Researchers fear that America's favorite second-chance exam may be exacerbating the dropout problem. [Electronic version] *Time.* Retrieved April 28, 2006, from http://www.time.com/time/magazine/printout/0,8816,1182430,00.html.

Thrasher, S. P., & Mowbray, C. T. (1995). A strengths perspective: An ethnographic study of homeless women with children. *Health and Social Work, 20,* (2), 93–96.

Tisdell, E. J. (1993). Feminism and adult learning: Power, pedagogy, and praxis. *New Directions for Adult and Continuing Education, 57,* 91–103.

Torres, C. A. (1995). Participatory action research and popular education in Latin America. In P. McLaren & J. M. Giarelli (Eds.), *Critical theory and educational research.* Albany: State University of New York Press.

Traub, J. (2006, October 8). The way we live now: 10–08–06; Pay for good behavior? *New York Times.* Retrieved November 5, 2006, from http://select.nytimes.com/search/restricted/article?res=FA0B11FC3F540C7B8CDDA9099.

Tuhus-Dubrow, R. (2004, March 25). Women and prison. *The Nation.* Retrieved January 18, 2007, from http://www.thenation.com/doc/20040412/tuhusdubrow.

Tyler, J. (2001). *What do we know about the economic benefits of the GED: A synthesis of the evidence form recent research.* Providence, R.I.: Brown University, National Bureau of Economic Research. [Electronic version] www.brown.edu/Departments/Education/facpages/j_tyler/PDF/what_do_we_know.pdf.

Tyler, J., Murnane, R., & Willett, J. (1999). Estimating the labor market signaling value of the GED. *The Quarterly Journal of Economics, 115,* (2), 431–68.

Tyler, J. H. (2001). *The economic benefits of the GED: A research synthesis.* Cambridge, Mass.: National Center for the Study of Adult Literacy and Learning, Harvard University.

Tyler, J. H. (2001). *So you want a GED? Estimating the impact of GED on the earnings of dropouts who seek the credential.* Cambridge, Mass.: National Center for the Study of Adult Literacy and Learning, Harvard University.

Tyler, J. H. (2005). *Evidence from Florida on the labor market attachment of male dropouts who attempt the GED.* Cambridge, Mass.: National Center for the Study of Adult Literacy and Learning, Harvard University.

United States Department of Education. (1990). *Education for homeless adults: The first year.* Washington, D.C.: U.S. Government Printing Office.

United States Department of Education. (1998). *Adult education for the homeless: A program in jeopardy.* Washington, D.C.: Division of Adult Education and Literacy, Office of Vocational and Adult Education. (ERIC Document Reproduction Service No. ED 429 233).

United States Senate. (2005). Senate Report 109-103. Departments of Labor, Health, and Human Services, and Education, and Related Agencies Appropriation Bill, 2006. Retrieved July 26, 2005, from http://thomas.loc.gov/cgi-in/cpquery/?&db_id=cp109FXZY6&r_n=sr103.109&item=&sel=TOC_856904&.

United States Senate Committee on Finance (2005). *Bipartisan welfare reform moves closer to law.* News Release, Max Baucus, Ranking Member. Retrieved March 9, 2005, from http://finance.senate.gov.

University of Massachusetts-Boston (1998). *A profile of housing in Massachusetts.* Boston: Donahue Institute, Citizen's Housing and Planning Association, University of Massachusetts-Boston.

University of Massachusetts-Boston (2000). *Situation critical: Meeting the housing needs for lower income Massachusetts residents.* Boston: Center for Social Policy, McCormack Institute, University of Massachusetts-Boston.

U.S. Fed News. (2005, March 3). Sen. Santorum rolls out Senate Republican poverty alleviation agenda. Retrieved May 25, 2005, from http://knowledgeplex.org.news/76738.html?p=1.

Usher, R., Bryant, I., & Johnston, R. (1997). *Adult education and the postmodern challenge.* London: Routledge.

Valdes, G. (1996). *Con respeto: Bridging the distances between culturally diverse families and schools.* New York: Teachers College Press.

Wallerstein, N. (1983). *Language and culture in conflict: Problem-posing in the ESL classroom.* Don Mills, Ontario: Addison-Wesley. (ERIC Document Reproduction Service No. 221 043).

Walsh, C. E. (Ed.). (1991). *Literacy as praxis: Culture, language, and pedagogy.* Norwood, N.J.: Ablex Publishing.

Way, N. (1998). *Everyday courage: The lives and stories of urban teenagers.* New York: New York University Press.

Weiler, K. (1988). *Women teaching for change: Gender, class, & power.* Westport, Conn.: Bergin & Garvey.

Weiler, K. (1994). Freire and a feminist pedagogy of difference. In P. McLaren & C. Lankshear (Eds.), *Politics of liberation: Paths from Freire.* New York: Routledge.

Weiler, K., & Mitchell, C. (Eds.). (1992). *What schools can do: Critical pedagogy and practice.* Albany: State University of New York Press.

Weis, L. (Ed.). (1988). *Class, race & gender in American education.* Albany: State University of New York Press.

Welch, S. D. (1985). *Communities of resistance and solidarity: A feminist theology of liberation.* Maryknoll, N.Y.: Orbis Books.

Wen, P. (2006, December 17). Job applicants face query on welfare, employers could receive tax credit. *Boston Globe.*

Wen, P. (2007, January 15). Job program for welfare recipients fall flat, employers say woes outweigh state subsidies. *Boston Globe.*

White, C., Ziegler, M., and Bingman, B. (1998). Families first: Implications of welfare reform for Tennessee adult basic education. Unpublished paper presented at the National Center for the Study of Adult Learning and Literacy's conference, Rutgers University, July 19–21, 1998.

Wikelund, K. R. (1993). *Motivations for learning: Voices of women welfare reform participants.* Philadelphia: National Center on Adult Literacy. (ERIC Document Reproduction Service No. ED 364 748.)

Williams, L. (1996). First enliven, then enlighten: Popular education and the pursuit of social justice. *Sociological Imagination, 33,* (2), 94–116.

Willis, P. (1977). *Learning to labor: How working class kids get working class jobs.* New York: Columbia University Press.

Wilson, W. J. (1987). *The truly disadvantaged.* Chicago: University of Chicago Press.

Wilson, W. J. (1996). *When work disappears: The world of the new urban poor.* New York: Knopf.

Winerip, M. (2003, August 13). The zero dropout miracle: Alas! Alack! A Texas tall tale. *New York Times.*

Wink, J. (1997). *Critical pedagogy: Notes from the real world.* White Plains, N.Y.: Longman Publishers.

Withorn, A. (1999). *Not for lack of trying: The struggle over welfare reform in Massachusetts, 1992–1998.* Boston: McCormack Institute, University of Massachusetts-Boston.

Withorn, A., & Jons, P. (1999). *Worrying about welfare reform: Community-based agencies respond.* Boston: University of Massachusetts-Boston.

Yoho, D. (2005, January 6). Job Training Improvement Act. Message posted to http://aaace-nla@lists.literacytent.org.

Young, M., Fleischman, H., Fitzgerald, N., & Morgan, M. (1994). *National evaluation of adult education programs: Patterns and predictors of client attendance.* Arlington, Va.: Development Associates.

Young, E., & Padilla, M. (1990). Mujeres unidas en accion: A popular education process. *Harvard Educational Review, 60,* (1), 1–17.

Zaharlick, A. (1992). Ethnography and anthropology and its value for education. *Theory Into Practice, 31,* (2), 116–25.

Zinn, H. (2003). *A people's history of the United States: 1492–present.* New York: Perennial Classics.

INDEX

LORNA RIVERA is an associate professor of sociology and community studies in the College of Public and Community Service at the University of Massachusetts, Boston.

The University of Illinois Press
is a founding member of the
Association of American University Presses.

Composed in 9.5/12.5 Trump Mediaeval LT Std
at the University of Illinois Press
Manufactured by Cushing-Malloy, Inc.

University of Illinois Press
1325 South Oak Street
Champaign, IL 61820-6903
www.press.uillinois.edu